Weeds of the Mind

How to Make New the Landscape of Your Thinking

Aaron Maners

Weeds of the Mind
Aaron Maners

Aaron Maners Ministries
Orlando, FL

Library of Congress Control Number: 2014903075

Copyright © 2014 Aaron Maners
ISBN: 978-1-940243-29-0

All rights reserved. No part of this book may be reproduced without written permission from the publisher or copyright holder, except in the case of brief quotations embodied in critical articles and reviews. No part of this book may be transmitted in any form or by any means—electronic, mechanical, photocopy, recording, or other—without prior written permission from the publisher or copyright holder.

Unless otherwise indicated, all Scripture quotations designated (NIV) are taken from the Holy Bible, New International Version® NIV® Copyright © 1973, 1978, 1984, 2011 by Biblica, Inc.® Used by permission. All rights reserved worldwide.

Unless otherwise indicated, all Scripture quotations designated (NIV) are taken from the Holy Bible, New International Version® NIV® Copyright © 1978 by New York International Bible Society.® Used by permission. All rights reserved worldwide.

Scripture taken from The Message. Copyright © 1993, 1994, 1995, 1996, 2000, 2001, 2002. Used by permission of NavPress Publishing Group.
The KJV is public domain in the United States.

Scripture quotations taken from the Amplified® Bible, copyright © 1954, 1958, 1962, 1964, 1965, 1987 by The Lockman Foundation. Used by permission.(www.Lockman.org)

Scripture taken from the New King James Version®. Copyright © 1982 by Thomas Nelson, Inc. Used by permission. All rights reserved.

Excitement About
Weeds of the Mind

"Aaron Maners tackles some of the most pressing issues the emerging generation is facing. His personal stories and disarming tone set readers up to truly engage his ideas in a big way. I believe this book will help a lot of people. Aaron is a colleague I am happy to call 'friend.'"

      Matt Keller; author, *God of the Underdogs*, www.MattKellerOnline.com
      Ft. Myers, FL

"Prayerfully, we won't be seen as too prejudiced in endorsing this book and its author in that Aaron is our son. The spiritual maturity in this book and in his preaching/teaching ministry distinguish Aaron as a man far beyond his years. Readers will enjoy the humor throughout 'Weeds,' but will also be challenged to think like a true child of God."

      Doug and Judy Maners
      Ekklesia Ministries, Orlando, FL

"A victorious life starts with right thinking. Aaron has done a masterful job at communicating how we can think at a new level. This is such a practical and authentic book on how to renew our minds and live at the level God intends for each us. This book will truly change your life if you apply the principles found within!"

J. Ashley Jensen, Lead Pastor
Victorious Church, Phoenix, AZ

"Weeds . . . no one likes them! I've found that if you don't control weeds in your life they will one day overtake you. Aaron has done us a huge favor by brilliantly exposing these weeds of the mind and motivating us to pull them out with a vengeance."

Scott George, Lead Pastor
Pinecastle United Methodist Church
Cofounder, Community Food & Outreach,
Orlando, FL

"Within minutes of picking up this book, I was confronted with gospel truths that challenged my thinking as a pastor, husband, and father. Aaron's creativity brings to life the biblical answers for the weeds of the mind we all encounter."

Bryan Lamoureux, Lead Pastor
Reverb Church, St. Augustine, FL

"'Weeds of the Mind' will have you rethinking the thoughts you have allowed to grow in your mind. Through his simple, conversational style, Aaron shows you how to weed out dangerous mindsets and replace them with seeds that will transform your future."

Eric Partin, Lead Pastor
Shoreline Church, Destin, FL

"Aaron does a masterful job using a common parable about yard work to illustrate the weeds that grow up in our minds and life and how we should be busy allowing God's Word and the Holy Spirit to pull them out and eliminate them."
> Larry Linkous, Lead Pastor
> New Life Christian Fellowship,
> Titusville, FL

"Aaron Maners has hit a homerun! 'Weeds of the Mind' is a revealing, practical, and insightful look at the greatest enemy to a successful future: our own thinking! This book is a game changer!"
> Ron Johnson, Lead Pastor
> One Church, Longwood, FL

"When I think of Aaron Maners and 'Weeds of the Mind,' I am reminded that this book is worth reading simply because Aaron Maners himself is more resilient than a weed. You'll love this book!"
> Gregg Johnson, Founder of J12 Ministries
> Anaheim, California

Dedication

This simple project is dedicated to everyone who has struggled to reconcile their thought patterns with the way they know they ought to live.

Always remember, Jesus is our answer.

Gratitude

A HUGE *thank you* to my amazing family for their healthy doses of support, patience, and encouragement. Suzy, Katie, Sarah, and Allie; I love you all.

I honor my parents and my brother and offer them gratitude for creating such a wonderful and life-giving environment in which to grow up.

Thank you to my amazing assistant, Lisa Pennington. Your heart to serve Jesus by serving us is making an impact that is truly changing lives.

My ministry is but a dim reflection of the men I have had the privilege to call "fathers in ministry." There are too many to count, but the margins of my Bible are wonderfully marked up with thoughts and impressions I was able to capture while sitting under your influence. Thank you for saying yes to your calling.

Table of Contents

Foreword — xiii

Chapter 1: My Beautiful Lawn — 1

Chapter 2: The Silent Invasion — 9

Chapter 3: Strategy for a Coup D'état — 21

Chapter 4: How to Win with Forgiveness — 35

Chapter 5: Winning Over Worry — 47

Chapter 6: Winning Over Our Will — 63

Chapter 7: Thinking for a Change — 73

Chapter 8: The Truth about You — 89

Foreword

Have you ever exclaimed, "What was I thinking?" If you have or have heard others say this, it usually follows some negative result in someone's life that they realize could have been averted by better thinking. No one ever has something wonderful happen and then blurt out, "What was I thinking?" What does that statement emphasize? This truth becomes evident: Your thoughts are taking you somewhere.

There is no such thing as idle thinking. Your thoughts are either taking you back to someplace you don't want to go or moving you forward to some victorious outcome.

The goal of every believer's life should be the result of 2 Corinthians 10:4-6, "for the weapons of our warfare are not physical [weapons of flesh and blood], but they are mighty before God for the overthrow and destruction of strongholds, [inasmuch as we] refute arguments and theories and reasonings and every proud and lofty thing that sets itself up against the [true] knowledge of God; and we lead every thought and purpose away captive into the obedience of Christ" (AMP). This is a great and most necessary goal if we are going to experience the life Christ has designed for us.

This book will help you reach this high place in your thought life and become transformed, "by the renewing of your mind" (Romans 12:2, NIV), resulting in victorious living. Aaron Maners does a masterful job, using a common parable about yard work to illustrate the weeds that grow up in our minds and lives, and how we should consistently allow God's Word and the Holy Spirit to pull them out and eliminate them.

I have known Aaron Maners from his earliest ministry years. We were blessed to have him serve on our ministry staff for eight years, leading a most explosive youth revival and was one of the first youth pastors to implement what has become known as the "Youth Church" model, now used by many churches around our nation. Aaron endeared himself to our hearts through his loyalty, commitment, and passion for Christ and God's people. I'm thrilled to have Aaron share the truths in this book and am confident we will all be clearer in our thinking and more victorious in our thought life because of the tools he gives us in *Weeds of the Mind*.

Author of *Don't Grow Weary*, and host of the nationally syndicated radio show "The Morning Drive," Dr. Larry Linkous has a contagious passion for life and is consumed with seeing people come into relationship with Jesus. He is committed to preaching the message of grace and how it relates to salvation and Christian maturity. Larry and his beautiful wife, Sandra, founded New Life Christian Fellowship (www.findnewlife.com) in Titusville, Florida in 1983.

Chapter One

MY BEAUTIFUL LAWN

A book about weeds?
The inspiration for this book came from a very unique place. It all started one day when I was performing the dreaded household chore of pulling weeds.

Just a few days before, on a random summer day in North Florida, my lovely wife, Suzy, and I had returned home from the grocery store. Like many of us men do, I had grossly overloaded my arms with way too many plastic bags, hoping this would help me avoid having to make a second trip back out to the car. The bags were ripping and tearing, and items were falling through the ripped bottoms. So intent was I on avoiding that second trip, I found myself trying to justify leaving four tomatoes and a box of toothpaste out in the yard until morning. I was lazy, I was tired, and I wanted to crash on the couch until dinner.

However, I went back out anyway. As I stepped out into the front yard and onto my nicely manicured outdoor "carpet" of St. Augustine grass, I suddenly saw something so horrifying that I abandoned the rescue of the tomatoes and toothpaste. I moved in closer to investigate. Sure enough. Evil strangers had set up shop in my yard. There were not just a few . . . they were "Legion." If I spotted one, I spotted hundreds. They were squatters. They weren't invited. They seemed to have a strategy that was silent and slow, but serious and determined. I was completely surrounded.

I yelled to my wife: "Suzy, we are being invaded!" Our beautiful yard had become another suburban statistic . . . we had been overrun by weeds.

I became a man on a mission. I thought, *These suckers want to take over my beautiful lawn!* I cleared my schedule for the upcoming Saturday and made myself ready to do battle. I put on my favorite camo shorts, tank top, flip-flops, and ball cap and smeared SPF 1000 all over my back and neck. I went back out to the spot where I had first seen them, put on my headphones, and with the help of some old Eagles tunes ("Already Gone" especially), I began pulling up weeds.

One hour turned into nearly six. The pile of weeds and debris grew bigger and bigger. So big, in fact, that it became clear I would not be able to celebrate my conquest that day. Instead, I started feeling a bit overwhelmed. The weeds were winning. My fingers hurt, my brain was fried, and the sun was going down. The project would require another day of effort.

It was in these few days of hard work, bent over beneath the brutal Florida sun, that I was able to sort of step outside the many pressures of life and dull thoughts that typically occupied my mind as I performed mundane tasks. Though I was busily working and focused heavily on my laborious chore, God was able to use it as an opportunity to speak to me.

Occasionally, God speaks to us in the oddest places, at the most obscure times. Isn't that wild?

Over the course of the great amount of time I spent with those crafty plants, God allowed me to gather a number of observations related to weeds. I drew parallels between the characteristics and operation of weeds and the way unhealthy thoughts and thoughts "not of God" creep in and pollute, infiltrate, and invade the minds of believers. The influence of the world, the challenges that affect us in life, and the way the enemy lies to us and tries to deceive us are all indicators that our minds need to be renewed and redeemed. All of us have dealt with this in one form or another, whether through times of unbelief, bitterness, unforgiveness, fear, or suspicion (to name just a few).

Simply put, just as weeds invade our yard, weeds of the mind invade our thoughts.

Though the enemy tries to pollute and crowd our thinking in order to get us off track in life, God always wins. He is continuously developing his amazing promises and blessings in us.

(You didn't really think this was a book about lawn maintenance, did you?)

God makes promises.

God's promises are the stuff from which great lives are made.

This brings to my memory the many times God blessed humankind in Scripture, and all the instances when he said things like, "be strong and courageous" and "do not be afraid." He isn't shy about telling us of his undying love for us and all the ways he has lavished it upon us. It is important to him that we remember and meditate on what he teaches us of the kingdom of heaven. He has allowed us to peek behind the curtain of the eternal.

Yet he cares about how we are living now.

Jesus said, *"Every plant that My heavenly Father has not planted will be (needs to be) pulled up"* (Matthew 15:13, NIV).

In God's eyes, "every plant" that is not of him needs to be pulled up. Even if we don't see them, don't feel the effects of their presence in the yards of our minds, or have grown accustomed to them being there, God has some heavy-duty landscaping scheduled for us.

So, what does the yard of your mind look like?

We have help in the process.

As you read this book, I encourage you to be entirely honest with yourself and ready for God to speak to you. Slow down for a bit and really take some time to evaluate your thoughts and thought patterns. Do they reflect God's heart and his ways, or do they mirror the world and its ways? While God cares about growing us and continuing to develop his character in us, the enemy cares only about distracting us and keeping us from a healthy relationship with our creator.

This reflection and evaluation might take some work because often we grow so used to wrong ways of thinking that they become a part of our lives. We get so deeply invested in our current way of thinking that we accept as "normal" some things God would like to see renewed and renovated. Even though he loves each of us unconditionally, he gets joy as we continue to develop Christlike traits and look more and more like him.

To do this, above all, you will need an overarching openness of heart.

There are three fundamental, essential elements for gaining the full benefit of this book. First, you will need the help of the Holy Spirit. God has provided his Holy Spirit to search your heart and speak directly to you the way he would have you go.

"Search me, O God, and know my heart; test me and know my anxious thoughts. See if there is any offensive way in me, and lead me in the way everlasting" (Psalm 139:23-24, NIV1984).

"In the same way, the Spirit helps us in our weakness. We do not know what we ought to pray for, but the Spirit himself intercedes for us with groans that words cannot express. And he who searches our hearts knows the mind of the Spirit, because the Spirit intercedes for the saints in accordance with God's will" (Romans 8:26-27, NIV).

Since the Spirit knows us intimately—our thoughts and feelings—he is able to work on the Father's behalf to open our eyes to things that are not pleasing to him.

Second, you will need to read the Bible and immerse yourself in all the important truths God uses to communicate his heart to you. The Word is timeless and speaks to all humankind from every angle so that we know what God cares most about doing in us.

Third, you will need to pray. God opens the door wide for us to pray to him. It is in the intimate place of prayer that he communicates with us. Prayer is a conversation and conversation creates relationship.

The Bible says that our thoughts define us.
You and I know our thoughts and thought patterns. We know the good, the bad, and the ugly. Right?

The Bible says, *"For as he thinketh in his heart, so is he"* (Proverbs 23:7, KJV). Oftentimes in Scripture, the word "mind" is translated as the "heart of a man." Did you notice the verse also includes the word "thinks"? It's easy to draw this conclusion and rephrase the verse: "as a man thinks in his mind, so is he."

I'm pretty sure there will have to be some sort of photo of me on the back of this book. In that photo, I will probably be dressed to impress, clean-shaven, and have a reasonable haircut in order to attain a modicum of presentability. The way I look in that photo is supposed to help you determine a few things about me—form a positive impression. However, that picture gives you only a glimpse of me. Though you will be able to make a few minor determinations from that limited information, you will not know everything about me, my life, my lifestyle, my strengths, my weaknesses, or my dreams and ambitions. Those deeper qualities and characteristics of who I am can only be found in one place . . . in my heart and mind. In spite of all that I do to express them through words and actions, I still do not fully disclose everything about me.

Only two people know me in full: me and God. This is an intense truth and it carries a lot of weight.

Again, *"For as he thinketh in his heart, so is he"* (Proverbs 23:7, KJV). We are ultimately fully defined by how we think. Because only God knows us, we must welcome him into this process. After all, he already knows it all. He has already accepted us and chosen to love us unconditionally. Best of all, he knew exactly what he was getting into when he sent his Son, Jesus, to die for our sins. God is "all in" when it comes to you and me. He is ready to receive us just as we are, but he also has every intention of developing his ways in us.

This should inspire some sort of reverence in how we navigate our thought life. It is a gargantuan, sobering thought that we will have to stand before him and give an account for the "real" us one day.

Are unwelcome invaders trying to creep into your thought life? Has any deception established a stronghold that is negatively affecting the way you think? Have your thoughts led to wrong actions and difficulties in relationships?

If so, it's not too late for you! It's never too late! At any time, in any season of life, we can take a moment to pray and ask the Holy Spirit to show us anything he needs to do to help us. (Isn't that great?) He is so faithful to work on our behalf. His greatest excitement is in continuing to mold you and me into the image of Jesus Christ. He has promised to remain faithful until that is completed! (See Philippians 1:6, NIV.)

Take a moment and pray this prayer: *"Lord, I submit myself to you right now. Please help me to see anything—any thinking patterns—that are not of you. Show me things that I have grown used to that tend to smother or crowd out the promises of God. Let me see anything that subtracts from the life of victory that has been promised to me by Christ. Work in my through this simple book. In Jesus' name I pray. Amen."*

Join me on this adventure. Go put on your camo shorts, your tanktop and your flip-flops and let's go get our hands dirty.

Chapter Two

THE SILENT INVASION

You wake up, put on your bathrobe, brew a pot of coffee, and walk out your front door to get the newspaper. As you let out a big yawn and enjoy a satisfying stretch from the safety of your porch, you get the feeling that you are being watched. It's creepy.

Maybe it's old man Miller, two houses over. Maybe it's that sweet little old lady with eleven cats, looking at you through binoculars . . . again. Nope. It's worse than that.

You are being watched by hundreds, possibly thousands of weeds. They are right in front of you. They snuck in stealthily and made your yard their new home, hidden amidst the good, healthy grass. Perhaps you looked right past them, never acknowledging their presence, but they ARE there, and they have an agenda. If left alone or unchecked, they will take over.

Nobody likes weeds. As far as choices for ground cover go, most of us prefer well-manicured, uniform grass. We water it and fertilize it in order to maintain the look we desire. Grass is the standard. Weeds are the enemy. Grass is the benchmark. Weeds have long been a most hated villain because in order for them

9

to have a fighting chance at survival, they have to invade that which is healthy, good, and well fed.

The same goes for weeds of the mind. We all have thoughts and thought patterns that hang out in our thinking that do not belong there or line up with what God says about us. These thoughts are bent on invasion.

I'm going to help you see how the enemy works, show you many things God has promised you, and ultimately, how you can receive and benefit from those promises in the context of a victorious life, through Christ Jesus. In the next few pages, you will learn some characteristics of weeds, how they attempt to infiltrate healthy yards, and some parallel characteristics of wrong thoughts and the potential damage they can cause.

One: Weeds work in groups and partner with other types of weeds.

Have you ever bent down to pull up a single weed that caught your eye and up with it came a whole hoard of additional weeds you had not seen? They were connected and holding onto each other for dear life. Ugh. A seemingly simple task has suddenly become gigantic!

They understand the dynamic that there is strength in numbers! Weeds seem to work in groups and partner with other types of weeds in order to create a strong, widespread network. They spider out, creating a web-like, sprawling system that covers the yard, maximizing their potential to find water, sunlight, and nutrients in the ground. Of course, these are the same things required by the good grass in the yard to remain healthy. Weeds tend to consume these things at the expense of the good grass and health of the yard.

The same principles hold true for the weeds of the mind. Often these weeds are deployed as an attack from the enemy. They are a spiritual attack meant to distract us and get our focus off of Christ, His blessings, and God's promises—to keep us from living victorious lives. Trust me, I write this from experience. Time and time again I have fallen for these attacks and distractions; hook, line, and sinker.

These thoughts tend to work hand in hand, thriving on the confusion in our lives. How can this be? It does seem contradictory, but we are judging this concept from the perspective of valuing order. God is a God of order, not of bewilderment and chaos.

These kinds of thoughts value confusion and disorder. Their agenda is never life-giving or based on truth or positive promises. They never build or bring healthy growth but only spoil and destroy.

This goes all the way back to the Garden of Eden. The serpent's strategy was to try and influence Eve by merely planting the seed of doubt about God's instructions and intentions. He understands that to wreak massive destruction, he does not have to do much more than sow a small seed of doubt that causes us to question God's goodness or care for our lives.

It only takes a seed—a single small seed. Why? Simply because seeds grow and multiply. It's in a seed's nature to grow once it is planted. It will mature and produce fruit of some sort, and all too often, the enemy capitalizes on this.

God's promises and truth develop a foundation for right thinking in our lives. The enemy counters this by presenting an ever-increasing network of wrong thoughts, based on doubt, lies, fear, or worry in order to derail us from healthy thinking.

At some point in your life, have you ever suffered significant emotional wounding by someone—been hurt deeply? Have you ever been a victim of a business deal gone bad? Has someone you trusted ever blatantly lied to you? Have you had a marriage fail for any number of difficult reasons? These things are hard and undoubtedly have a dramatic effect on us emotionally. These and many other kinds of traumatic offenses often produce seeds of wrong thinking.

You may find yourself unable to get over such offenses. Why? Something was planted and it grew. Maybe it grew up along with other negative or traumatic events you didn't count on. Perhaps your short-term anger actually linked up with unforgiveness and resentment and developed into a mistrust of others. Over time, it linked up with a prejudice, and eventually you find yourself living an exclusionary lifestyle, feeling alone, and even depressed. All of this is sure to affect who you are and how you live life. It can effectively snowball out of control and create a destructive, toxic lifestyle. This isn't God's plan and is not how we were created to live.

Time to clean the house.

It is so important that we stay vigilant and remain on the alert against thinking like this. We can never be effective in this strictly through our own power. We MUST rely on the Holy Spirit and on what God's Word says about us in order to be effective.

Jesus warned a crowd of people of the danger of spiritual attacks and how great a negative effect they can have.

"When an evil spirit comes out of a man, it goes through arid places seeking rest and does not find it. Then it says, 'I will return to the house I left.' When it arrives, it finds the house is unoccupied, swept clean and put in order. Then it goes and takes with him seven other spirits more wicked than itself, and they go in and live there. And the final condition of that man is worse than the first" (Matthew 12:43-45, NIV1984).

God is still interested in "sweeping the house clean" and "putting it in order" in each of our lives. He cares that we are free from the tormenting influences and voices that plague so many of us. As he does this work in our lives, it's important that we begin to "occupy" the house with the ways of thinking that bring glory to God.

If you've had struggles with abandonment and loneliness, he can cause you to feel loved and accepted. If you've dealt with guilt and shame, he can show you what true love really looks like. If you are having a hard time shaking the "scarlet letters" of your past, he can begin to assure you that you are made new and established as righteous in God's eyes.

One of my favorite authors, Francis Frangipane, writes: "If you want to identify the hidden strongholds in your life, you need only survey the attitudes in your heart. Every area in your thinking that glistens with hope in God is an area which is being liberated by Christ. But any system of thinking that does not have hope, which feels hopeless, is a stronghold which must be pulled down."[1]

Two: An individual weed may have a short life span but it can distribute hundreds of seeds in that time.

Seeds grow. We cannot minimalize or trivialize the power of a seed.

I know men who curse the day that they first saw a pornographic image because it resulted in a long-term struggle with pornography addiction that they grew to despise. I know women who allowed one person's inconsiderate insult to determine their eating habits and poor self-image. These started as seeds—small but potentially dangerous.

King David said, *"I will set no worthless thing before my eyes; I hate the work of those who fall away; it shall not fasten its grip on me"* (Psalm 101:3, NAS). At some point, King David had a realization that it brought pleasure to God when he hated sin and carefully crafted his life to abstain from it and never allow it an entrance into his life. Chronologically, David wrote the thoughts captured in Psalm 101 quite some time after his life altering sexual affair with Bathsheba, as he was preparing the kingdom to be handed over to

Solomon. It sounds like the musings of a man who has failed, repented, and learned his lesson well.

We do know that David wanted to rule righteously as king in order to honor God. That's the big picture. However, the lesson and principle go much deeper and intimate than that. Sure, he wanted to be a righteous king so that God was glorified, but he was still a man, a man who wanted to bring glory to God with the most basic and specific of actions. This gives us a bit more of a glimpse into who he was. His heart was inherently pure. After all, David is forever known in Scripture as being *"a man after God's own heart."*

Some time ago, a friend and I attended a men's retreat at a campground in the Florida countryside. The guest minister spoke about purity in our thought life. He said so many things over the course of that weekend that were strong and made a strong impression on us. However, I most clearly remember a line from his own story that left an indelible mark on me: "If I'd have known the magnitude of the struggle I would have in my thirties and forties, I'd never have looked at those pornographic images when I was just twelve and thirteen."

He didn't articulate these next few thoughts, but I feel I can summarize the types of things that he may well have cried out: "God, I promise that was the last time! God, why can't I win over this? How do I shake this repulsive addiction?" In Psalm 13:2, David penned a similar emotional cry to the Lord: *"How long will I wrestle with my thoughts and every day have sorrow in my heart? How long will my enemy triumph over me?"* (NIV1984).

the silent invasion 15

The story that retreat speaker told has an intensity to it because it deals with the impact of pornographic influence. Our society is bombarded with sexual images daily. Not long ago, a study conducted to explore the impact of pop culture, particularly sex television, revealed that adultery and premarital sex were both highly glorified. Melissa Henson, the director for the Parents Television Council, in a recent interview with *The Christian Post* expounds on the dynamics involved in this.

> Whether we choose to admit it or not, television is profoundly influential. On some level whether conscious or unconscious, people who watch a lot of television come to view the lives they see on television as somehow truer, or more real, or more representative of "the real world." When folks see adultery or sexual promiscuity depicted as normative on television, they come to believe that it is more common in the real world than it actually is. That, in turn, translates into a type of pressure by removing moral or cultural barriers that might have prevented an individual from engaging in those kinds of behaviors.[2]

Don't get me wrong. I like watching television. However, it is important to be selective in choosing which shows to watch. We must be diligent in this because shows we watch on television plant seeds in our minds and affect our home environment, positively or negatively.

Three: If weeds aren't dealt with, not only will they invade and infect your lawn, they will spread to other lawns around you.

Maybe you live next door to that kind of neighbor who doesn't spend quite as much time on the maintenance of his yard as you do. Maybe you drop subtle hints to him about the unkempt forest that is slowly growing in his front yard: "Hey Jim, why you wanna' do me like that? Do you wanna' borrow my lawnmower? Please?" Your concern is understandable; you have worked hard to create a space that is healthy and weed free and you are concerned that it is just a matter of time until his "out of control" wilderness works its way onto your investment of time and money.

The same can easily happen if we allow the offenses of others to creep over our own mental property line. Have you ever listened to someone's story of being offended and felt an element of empathy for them? Did you get to the point where you were as mad or hurt as they were and begin to carry their offense for the situation—even begin to treat the offender very differently?

I call that "offense piggybacking."

It's kind of like that bitter relative you have stay with you as a guest for Thanksgiving or Christmas. You feel obligated to let them use the guestroom for the holiday but you dread their time with the family because they constantly spew discontent and dredge up old stories that are full of bitterness and disgruntlement. You might say they arrived with three suitcases; one had clothes in it but the other two were full of drama!

When they arrive they start "unpacking" it all and the whole house begins to get that "funk" circulating around in it. They want you and everyone else to help them carry their umbrage and anger.

It's important that you not allow yourself to be influenced by them when it comes to their offense. You must stay true to being a model of Christ's reconciliation and forgiveness. You don't want to find yourself erring on the side of being judgmental and selective with your love rather than being life-giving. Don't let their weeds jump into your yard.

When we lived near Jacksonville, Florida, we had great neighbors. For eight years, we would talk and laugh in our driveways, watch each other's home when the other traveled, bring in the trashcans, and collect the mail, if needed. We got along wonderfully.

In the backyard, we shared a common privacy fence that was six feet high and covered with a Magnolia vine. It bloomed with little white flowers and smelled great. One day, I went back to that corner of the yard, and saw that I had neglected to trim the vine. Okay, truthfully, I had never trimmed that vine. It was out of control (reminding me of the movie, *The Blob*). The vine had totally taken over a small tree that was right on the fence line, all but killing it. It sent out dozens of vines onto the roof of my home and sent dozens more into the system of gutters at that corner of my home, and it was working its way into my neighbor's yard.

One problem was affecting two households.

I could no longer rationalize inaction or act like no one would ever see the problem. I had to be proactive and tackle the project right away. I spent more than one Saturday on that cluster of vines, hoping that my vines wouldn't do any further damage and harm a friendship.

We can affect others, and others can affect us.

Be proactive and take action.

"But clothe yourself with the Lord Jesus Christ (the Messiah), and make no provision for [indulging] the flesh [put a stop to thinking about the evil cravings of your physical nature] to [gratify its] desires (lusts)" (Romans 13:14, AMP). This is Paul's directive for Christian living and dealing with the issues of right thinking versus wrong and unhealthy thinking.

First, he instructs us to take action and clothe ourselves with Jesus—put him on, wear him. We are to walk around covered by him and allow people to see him on us. We are to let his very character permeate every facet of our lives.

How do we do that? We do it through the Word. Jesus is the Word and his very nature is expressed through it. *"In the beginning was the Word, and the Word was with God, and the Word was God. He was with God in the beginning. Through him all things were made; without him nothing was made that has been made. In him was life, and that life was the light of all mankind"* (John 1:1-4, NIV).

Secondly, he tells us to deny the flesh and wrong ways of thinking. He tells us to "make no provision" (no room) for anything that resembles the fleshly way of living. He is serious about our spiritual health and how it affects the rest of our lives. So should it be with us as believers.

Can you imagine if the global church lived in such a way that Christ was so exemplified and glorified? Can you imagine being a part of the impact that this would have on lost and hurting humanity?

Ask yourself these few questions:

- Am I thinking God's thoughts?
- What seed thoughts are active in my thinking processes?
- Am I giving in to temptation and entertaining unhealthy thoughts like doubt, lust, or unforgiveness?

Take a few moments and pray something like this: *"Holy Spirit, I need your help. Help me to see that which is not pleasing to you. Help me to identify all that is not of God, all that doesn't bring him glory. Please work in me supernaturally to renew my mind. Make Scripture and promises come alive in my life. Amen."*

Chapter Three

STRATEGY FOR A COUP D'ETAT

One day, I was on my knees pulling up crabgrass when a guy walked up to me. He was a big sweaty guy with the pants of his coveralls tucked into his knee-high boots. His crew cut allowed all the beads of perspiration to gather on his head. Some form of tobacco product in his mouth caused him to spit approximately every three or four sentences. His nametag said Lee (I'll never forget it) and he operated the truck I'd seen fertilizing yards in our neighborhood. A virtual cloud of chemical aroma surrounded the truck (or maybe just Lee).

Lee was nice enough, as most good ol' boys are. He had just pulled over to talk with me about the potential of retaining his services and becoming his newest client. I shook his hand and listened.

If you have ever spent any time with guys candidating to spray your lawn, you know they work hard to convince you that sneaky little weeds are the most evil things on earth. Each will tell you his own war stories and how he singlehandedly defeated the "big outbreak of '03" and saved untold acres of St. Augustine grass in helpless and hapless Florida retirement communities. (Yep, that was him.)

Perhaps Lee should wear a cape.

I listened to him for about twenty minutes primarily because he knew so much more about this than I did. He knew what kind of grass I had and what weeds would be most likely to invade. He knew what the characteristics of the weeds were and how they would accomplish the takeover. He assured me that the problem was going to grow to be so epic that surely the Apocalypse itself would happen right in my very own yard!

At this point, it is anti-climactic to tell you that I did not hire Lee and his "wondertruck" that day. I chose to deal with the weeds on my own and pull them myself. The idea of my dogs running around in chemically maintained ground cover didn't set right with me, so I went the natural route. However, I learned some things from Lee that day and became determined to win my war with weeds. The process would require an investment of many hours of my time, but it would be well worth it in the end. Besides, it was becoming increasingly apparent that God was trying to teach me a few things and he happened to be using this mundane, wearisome project to do so.

The solution was simple, on paper. I had to learn to spot the characteristics of weeds in order to deal with them and restore my yard to health. In other words, I needed to get the wrong things out and put the right things in.

Here are just a few of the "secret" characteristics of weed armies that help them accomplish their dastardly coup d'etats.

One: Weeds have the ability to grow on their own.

Weeds have never needed us. They have never needed our help. As a matter of fact, they actually thrive if they are left alone. After all, there has never been, to my knowledge, a weed fertilizer product sold down at the local hardware store. No one sells weed food. Weeds become a powerful force in our yards on their own and are doing just fine without our benevolent intervention.

Have you ever seen a weed grow out of a crack in the concrete? They are impressive little suckers. They seem to have the ability to push through even when the odds are stacked against them. Somehow, someway, they succeed.

However, in a lawn, weeds have access to all the soil, nutrients, and irrigation meant for the grass. In this context, they steal. They are the pickpockets of the lawn maintenance world.

In the same way that our healthy grass needs an environment that is weed free, well watered, and has nutrient rich soil, a healthy mind needs to be saturated with the promises of God and fed well by the Word. For example, think of someone who has a strong self-image. What are the factors that make them strong? What are their thinking processes? What negative obstacles are NOT present in their lives?

Have a healthy self-image from God.

For believers, one of the greatest contributing factors to developing a healthy and strong self-image is knowing who you are in Christ. It becomes the basis for a healthy identity. This was modeled for us by Jesus himself, as we see in John's Gospel: *"Jesus knew that the Father had put all things under his power, and that he had come from God and was returning to God; so he got up from the meal, took off his outer clothing, and wrapped a towel around his waist. After that, he poured water into a basin and began to wash his disciples' feet, drying them with the towel that was strapped around him"* (John 13:3-5, NIV).

A few things leap out to me from these verses. First, Jesus knew the Father had "put all things under his power," so nothing would be impossible for him. Nothing would take Jesus by surprise, defeat him, or cause him any panic. All of God's totality was handed right over to Jesus. (That would contribute greatly to anyone's confidence and security, for sure.)

Second, he knew that he had come "from God." He knew that his roots were in the Almighty. The same characteristics and attributes that define the Creator of the universe wrote the DNA code for Jesus. It wasn't merely about an address; it was about a lineage, a promise, and a pedigree.

Third, he knew that there was a promise that he would soon return "to God." There was anticipation and an excitement that once his mission to reconcile mankind was complete, he would head back to sit next to the Father.

These things helped produce a security and healthy self-image in Jesus that enabled him to wrap around himself the towel of a servant and begin washing the feet of the men who served him.

Those truths that we "know" become the things that we "think." So, what if we thought according to what we knew God has already spoken? What if his promises saturated our minds and registered deep into our hearts? Wouldn't our corresponding actions and lifestyles reflect more of him to a lost and dying world? Is it possible that our light would shine brighter?

Two: Weeds are sneaky.

Weeds are ninjas. They are quiet, stealthy and not at all interested in drawing attention to themselves. Oftentimes, they are present and in full force long before we really know they are there.

As a young boy, like most, I was fascinated with ninjas. I watched Bruce Lee movies repeatedly to see how these warriors of the shadows moved stealthily under the cover of night, scaled walls, climbed trees, and eliminated their objective. That is, until Bruce Lee got there just in time to wage shirtless war on dozens of highly trained dudes in their black pajamas. (Silly ninja, you got schooled by Bruce Lee . . . again!)

Back to the subject at hand . . . weeds. They seem to have the insatiable desire and unlimited ability to strangle healthy grass and take their spot in the ecosystem of your lawn quite quickly, unless someone recognizes their threat and chooses to do something about it.

The same goes with our thoughts. Oftentimes, we become aware of thoughts and trains of thought that capitalize upon a time when we were distracted, hurt, or weak. These seasons of life might have been so bad that they left us in a state of confusion and disorder.

Though some may well encourage us to pray, realistically, we just don't know how we ought to pray. Again, God has made provision for us in times just like this.

"In the same way, the Spirit helps us in our weakness. We do not know what we ought to pray for, but the Spirit himself intercedes for us with groans that words cannot express. And he who searches our hearts knows the mind of the Spirit, because the Spirit intercedes for the saints in accordance with God's will" (Romans 8:26-27, NIV).

Wow, the Holy Spirit "helps us in our weakness."

Even when we don't feel like a "Super Christian"? Even when we have messed up? Even when we are wrestling with an area of sin? Yes. He helps us with all our weak areas—even our thoughts.

This passage also says the Spirit "searches our hearts (minds)." God is continually doing maintenance and looking for areas of our lives in which he can help us. He's eager to assist us in our life changes and to strengthen us where the enemy has tried to sneak in and set up shop.

Three: Weeds have a structure and features similar to healthy grass.

In popular culture "doppelganger" is a term for a person who looks eerily similar to someone else. They are a twin, of sorts, with someone that they don't even know. There are some funny websites where people post pictures of average people who appear to be doppelgangers of famous celebrities. The results are quite comical. Heck, you may live next door to dude who looks just like Robert DeNiro!

There is an old saying: "If it looks like a duck, walks like a duck, and quacks like a duck . . . it must be a duck." However, that's not always the case, is it? Sometimes weeds are disguised and camouflaged so similarly that it is hard to distinguish between the invader and healthy blades of grass that rightfully belong in the yard.

One day, I was excited to have stumbled upon a cleverly hidden weed. I found myself talking to it: "I almost didn't see you." Even as I sit here and type these thoughts, I am thinking, *Aaron, you spend WAY too much time out in your yard!* Maybe it isn't really bad until you start hearing them talk back, right?

"I'm going to have to pull you up . . . you are dangerous."

"I'M NOT A WEED . . . I BELONG HERE."

"Hmmm, you are green . . . small—you do appear to be a plant . . . but something doesn't seem quite right. All the other good grass around you seems to be dying off."

(This is getting embarrassing now.)

There are times when we will have a wrong thought— a rogue thought—that tries to masquerade as a right thought. To know the difference we must learn how to measure thoughts against God's standards—his Word. After all, his Word is truth; it is unchanging and will always point us toward hope in Jesus.

I once heard an amazing speaker, Rick Reynolds, founder and president of Affair Recovery, owner of Crossroads Counseling in Austin, Texas. He mentioned an easy way to remember how to tell the difference

strategy for a coup d'etat

between right and wrong thinking: "Just remember 'L.I.F.E.'"

L Label

Label the rogue thought. Have the courage to call it what it is. Be bold and say (aloud, if necessary): "That's not from God. That doesn't match up with his Word or his promises for my life." This will help you to see when the enemy tries to use the same strategy again.

I Identify

Know that the enemy wants to try to resurrect the "old man" in you that Paul speaks of in 2 Corinthians 5:17, in order to make you think you are somehow less than saved. Be bold and say (aloud, if necessary): "That's not me. That's sin in me. I am a child of God." God has promised to form his character in you and to continue to craft you in his image.

At this point, you can also devalue the thought: "That is a stupid thought that would bring corresponding stupid behavior. THAT kind of thinking and THOSE kinds of actions will most certainly yield negative consequences." (To reinforce this, you might think of the consequences of such wrong thinking and actions from your past.)

F Focus

As believers, our focus needs to be on Jesus and the continual progression of his image being formed in us. Everything else is a potential distraction.

Ask yourself this poignant question, *"Do I want to be captured by THIS?"*

You were created for more than whatever is trying to take you down. Whatever captures your thought life captures you.

E Evaluate

Ask yourself these questions as you evaluate whether or not a thought is healthy and meets God's standards of what and how to think.

- If I were to dwell on this thought, would it bring life or death?
- Do these thoughts bring glory to God?
- Is this the voice of the Shepherd or the butcher?

Four: Weeds are a natural ground cover, just not what we want in our yard.

Did you ever stop and think that every weed is found in nature? Weeds were there first, right? In areas that are natural and undeveloped, weeds thrive and serve as the majority of the initial ground cover. Weeds happen naturally.

Consider yourself forewarned that your mind will be blown in these thirty-four short words: A yard is a redeemed plot of land that is planted with healthy seed for healthy grass. Until someone saw potential in it and began to rightly cultivate it, only wild weeds grew there.

The same holds true for our minds. Our unredeemed minds are a haven for weeds—anything goes. All sorts of methods of thinking were developed and flourished in them, but only those in accord with our old nature and worldly ways of thinking. Try as we might, not much good can come out of that environment, can it?

"Indeed, many of our opinions about life are ours only because we know of no other way to think."[3] When we come to Christ, our minds are redeemed and the process of renewal has begun. We need to guard ourselves against the "old nature/old man" way of thinking and the enemy's seed thoughts. (Actually, it's more like the whole spiritual landscaping crew needs to come in and start quite the landscaping project!)

> *For we know that our old self was crucified with him so that the body of sin might be rendered powerless, that we should no longer be slaves to sin—because anyone who has died has been freed from sin.*
>
> *Now if we died with Christ, we believe that we will also live with him. For we know that since Christ was raised from the dead, he cannot die again; death no longer has mastery over him. The death he died, he died to sin once for all; but the life he lives, he lives to God.*
>
> *In the same way, count yourselves dead to sin but alive to God in Christ Jesus. Therefore do not let sin reign in your mortal body so that you obey its evil desires. Do not offer the parts of your body to sin, as instruments of wickedness, but rather offer yourselves to God, as those who have been brought from death to life; and offer the parts of your body to him as instruments of righteousness. For sin shall not be*

your master, because you are not under law, but under grace. (Romans 6:6-14, NIV)

So, even with the understanding that the weeds were there first, things need to change. God takes what was undesirable and redeems it. He changes it to be representative of him. The "old" no longer runs the show, we are made new. In verse thirteen, Paul goes on to encourage us to stay alert and be cautious in how we live; how we utilize all that God has given us. We have to be good stewards of the new life we have in Christ, making sure we aren't letting anything back in that doesn't belong there.

Recently, I saw a documentary about the financial challenges faced by the city of Detroit. The film showed tons of footage of streets that were once bustling with commerce, now empty, spray painted and desolate. They showed windows broken, buildings condemned and vacated, and playgrounds overgrown with weeds, long since abandoned. The progression or "circle of life" had gone from being untouched, vacant land, to being redeemed by man for specific purposes and use, and then returning back to being overgrown with the same weeds that were once there in abundance.

It's interesting and somewhat inevitable.

Five: Weeds are determined, tenacious, and on a mission to take over the world (or MY yard, at least).

In my twenty or so years as a homeowner, I have seen seasons where weeds were more than able to overtake areas of my yard by killing everything in their path. Patches that were once green with grass were now replaced with various forms of weeds—something surely undesirable. Actually, it is in the weeds' best interest to eliminate all competition in order to attempt to guarantee furthering their own survival.

We have to be equally determined to have the mind of Christ and populate our minds with faith and faith-filled thinking. After all, we have to be on the lookout for weeds of unbelief and fear.

Do you remember the woman with the issue of blood Mark writes about in his Gospel, chapter 5? Jesus was surrounded by a gigantic crowd and spending time that day ministering to and healing the sick. The buzz in the streets must have been palpable and electric! Sure enough, a nameless woman who had endured twelve years of suffering heard the stories of a miracle worker and became determined to find him and receive her own story of relief and life change.

It's remarkable to note that after she heard about Jesus, the Bible says "she thought, 'If I just touch his clothes, I will be healed'" (Mark 5:28, NIV). Isn't that interesting? Her actions were rooted in her thought and her belief. It set the stage for her determined action of pressing through the crowd.

Oftentimes, our crises cause us to have to reach deep down into our tenacious faith, right? Intense prayer comes from this place. Intercession for others comes from this place. Like any muscle in our physical bodies, I believe our prayer "muscle" can be strengthened through exercise and that helps develop our faith! You too can be full of faith in your thinking and can use that to press through whatever challenge you face!

So, how well do you think in your crises? Where do you set the standard for your thoughts when the going gets rough? Does the problem get more attention or does Jesus' hemline?

Be determined. Be tenacious. Be strong in your faith.

In the next chapter, I am going to challenge you to live a lifestyle of forgiveness and learn to remove any residue of resentment or judgment from your life so you can live in true freedom. By doing this, your mind, your actions, and your lifestyle will shine the light of Jesus to the people you encounter.

Chapter Four

HOW TO WIN WITH FORGIVENESS

The Lindsey Parable
Let me tell you about Lindsey.

   Lindsey is a recently divorced woman in her early forties who is establishing her foothold in middle management in corporate America. She is known for her radiant smile, corny jokes, and belief that "a little Botox never hurt anyone." Oh, and she is hopelessly addicted to some of those singing competition shows. The joy of Lindsey's life is her absolutely boy crazy teenage daughter.

   Not long ago, Lindsey went out on her fifth date with a gentleman from the office where she works. She is wondering if she should get her hopes up because most guys seem to be "interested in only one thing" from her. On the surface, her life seems normal in many ways, but on the inside she wrestled with love and identity.

   At six years old, when every little girl should be crawling up into daddy's lap, Lindsey's dad decided to leave. He never called, never wrote . . . he just left. Mom took it very hard and medicated her pain with every bottle and boyfriend she could get her hands on. Lindsey spent a ton of time moving around from relative to relative, but never really felt that whatever

35

house she was currently in was "home." Everything had been turned upside down in her life. It didn't seem fair.

Early on, with tears in her eyes and extreme frustration in her heart, she made a decision that no one would hurt her and make her feel like her mother felt. She needed to be strong. Subconsciously she began to erect walls around herself and it affected every relationship thereafter.

As a teen and even into her twenties, Lindsey often traded away more than her affections for what she thought was love. Those "loves" always proved to be temporary. In her first marriage, she emerged from behind her walls long enough to be wounded deeply by James. When that relationship crashed and burned, she went back inside and locked up. This cycle had become all too familiar to her.

She became determined: "I've got to be stronger. I've got to protect myself." However, she knew that this strategy was dangerous and had no firm long-term foundation. Her wake-up call came when she saw the mirror image of herself and her habits acted out in her beautiful teenage daughter's promiscuity. Things had to change but she didn't know exactly how or even where to begin.

Some months ago, one of her coworkers invited her to a small study group where a few ladies were working through a book together and prayed for each other in a local coffee shop. It was casual and surprisingly comfortable. They were real. They were authentic. In the most sincere and simplistic ways, they shared the life-changing power of Jesus and his great love for people . . . people just like Lindsey.

Three weeks later, at the study, Lindsey asked Jesus into her heart.

As she grew as a Christian, Lindsey began praying things like most of us do: "Lord, make me more like you. Make my love more pure." However, her heartfelt prayers didn't seem to have the instant effect for which she hoped. She found that she was becoming more and more aware of the walls she had built up and that she had settled for cold love. The Holy Spirit revealed this as she developed new, healthy friendships.

She turned to Jesus and prayed: "Help me to identify those bitter roots of the past. Pull them up, Lord. Show me where these actions originated and how to deal with them. I know they do not reflect you or who you have created me to be."

Bit by bit, issue by issue, as the Lord began to bring memories and thoughts to Lindsey's mind, he instructed her to have a heart of forgiveness and release from any kind of judgment the ones who had hurt her. He also told her he would help her in this process and heal her heart.

Lindsey felt prompted by the Lord to sit down one morning and write two or three very important letters. These were letters of forgiveness and hard to write. She didn't know if she would even have the courage to mail them. Nevertheless, she wrote them as a gesture . . . as a prayer. It helped. It helped tremendously. As she wrote, God was able to take those moments to minister to her heart and help her release from judgment and condemnation the people who had hurt her (though she would later say that she was the one who was truly liberated).

Today, Lindsey is free from the bitterness and unforgiveness she had felt toward her father and mother, her old boyfriends, and even her ex-husband. She is free from the walls she had erected in order to protect herself that had actually came to isolate her more. Her love is stronger and more Christlike. She now models the right way of thinking. She walks in freedom and forgiveness as a healthy example to her daughter.

We like Lindsey.

"See to it that no one misses the grace of God and that no bitter root grows up to cause trouble and defile many" (Hebrews 12:15, NIV). Simply put, bitterness and unforgiveness cause all kinds of trouble and can pollute many parts of our lives . . . it really jacks things up.

Weeds must be pulled up by the roots.

I remember times when our girls were younger that I would spend weekends on yard projects, just as many suburban family guy types often have to do. After just a few minutes of being out in the sun, on my knees, by myself, I would invariably think, "I have three very capable daughters who could be out here helping me, but instead they are inside watching cartoons." Would I be disingenuous in denying I was looking for some bonding time? Correct. I actually wanted cheap child labor—and by cheap I mean free.

You can imagine what happened when I would step inside the house in the midst of my yard projects and yell, "*GIRLS!*" They ran, they hid, or they barricaded themselves in the bathroom. Instantaneously, they became the most skilled of negotiators, each armed with an uncanny ability to communicate excuses faster than a tommygun firing bullets in a gangster film. They knew what was coming and what I was going to ask of them. (Frankly, I know this placed my running for the "Father of the Year Award" in jeopardy more than once.)

Nevertheless, in each of those sessions with the girls, I made sure they understood that each weed needed to be rightly eradicated from the yard, i.e. pulled up by the roots. We couldn't merely pull the green, leafy tops off the weeds because with the root system intact, in just a few days, it would produce another leafy top and we would be right back at square one.

All plants have roots of some sort. They are the source of the plant's stability and strength, and they provide the way for the plant to obtain and process nutrients from the soil. Roots are also the place of origin where the seed initially landed and established residency. Where the roots go down, the plant dwells.

To get rid of weeds permanently you have to deal with the root. You might feel some immediate satisfaction by mowing over the weeds, but that will only mask the fact that their roots still exist. In due time, they will be back.

The same principle can be applied to wrong thinking in our lives. We cannot think we can merely wish away a thought process or dangerous thinking; we have to get to the root of the problem. We might need to ask ourselves tough questions like, *Why is that particular thought here?*

Where did it come from?

Someone near to our family who we knew very well had a very poor view of people of other races. He was a bigot and very hung up on the color of skin and origins of others. I'm not sure why. Things got so extreme that he would pack up and move out of a neighborhood if people of color moved in. Yet he actively served in his church in various leadership roles during his season of extremism. His thinking was not just a shame, but also his hypocrisy tarnished his family's name and reputation, and he risked his church's name and reputation as well. His wrong thinking caused great damage to his family, friends, and neighbors

Even as a kid, I would try to reconcile this in my mind and would ask, "Why is this? How does this begin? Where does it start?"

It would be entirely speculation for me at this point, but I wonder if this was an issue of him picking up this wrong way of thinking during his upbringing after hearing it from others in his family. Perhaps he had a negative experience like a fight or longstanding rivalry with a person of color when he was younger. Whatever was the reason or the root, the heart of God wants to deal with it and heal it so that the character of Christ is shown out of that lifestyle instead.

Make no mistake, bitter roots or unforgiveness that may have originated yesterday can clearly affect all aspects of our lives today. Something that WAS can create what currently IS.

It's not just a matter of desiring or even deciding to change the way we think. Our minds have long practiced their way of thinking and have formed deep roots in our brains that MUST be pulled up entirely. Lindsey's wrong behavior and actions were a result of her dysfunctional early home environment. What we see and experience through repetition eventually become what we dwell on, and eventually, what we act like.

We don't have to stay stuck there.

The good news is, we don't have to stay stuck there. The Bible says in Romans, *"The mind of sinful man is death, but the mind controlled by the Spirit is life and peace"* (Romans 8:6, NIV1984). If there are sinful or unhealthy strongholds in our lives, we will soon find that our minds are polluted with a dangerous way of thinking. Our goal must be to allow the Holy Spirit to change our thinking from a sinful, unloving, unforgiving flow to establish that which is Christlike and brings "life and peace."

Scripture also gives us a sort of list to set our minds on. These things are representative of the heart of God and give us a better understanding of how he wants us to spend our thinking energies and efforts: *"Finally, brothers and sisters, whatever is true, whatever is noble, whatever is right, whatever is pure, whatever is lovely, whatever is admirable—if anything is excellent or praiseworthy—think about such things"* (Philippians 4:8, NIV).

This might seem a bit unconventional, but I have a fun thing for you to do. Approach people who know both you and your parents well. Ask them if they notice traits in you that are the same as your parents. (Many people are certain they are NOTHING like their parents.)

- Ask them to comment on the way you say and articulate things.
- Ask them to observe the way you look while you talk—including your gestures and posture.
- What are some of your observable quirks?

Weeding is inconvenient and uncomfortable.

Weeding is inconvenient and uncomfortable. No news flash there, right? Who wants to do it anyway? I can't imagine anyone waking up on a Saturday morning and saying, *"Yahoo! I have to go spend several hours on my hands and knees, pulling weeds out of my lawn today!"* It's an amazing phenomenon that even at the prospect of pulling weeds, before we even make it to the door, we are able to find one million other things that are a higher priority for our time and attention. Saturday naps come to mind right away.

If you pull a weed up by the roots at first sight, there is a probability that it will be easier to extract simply because it hasn't had time to develop strong, steadfast roots. However, if you put it off due to inconvenience and procrastinate, the roots will have time to grow deeper, making it much harder to pull and eradicate.

A stronghold has a strong hold.

A weed establishes a stronghold by its roots. In other words, the deeper the roots, the stronger the stronghold. The same can be said of our thinking patterns. We could say it this way: A STRONGHOLD is an established way of thinking that began long ago and became part of our way of thinking. *"Some people . . . think that we live by the standards of this world. For though we live in the world, we do not wage war as the world does. The weapons we fight with are not the weapons of the world. On the contrary, they have divine power to demolish strongholds. We demolish arguments and every pretension that sets itself up against the knowledge of God, and we take captive every thought to make it obedient to Christ"* (2 Corinthians 10:2-5, NIV).

According to Paul's letter to the church in Corinth, even if we have strongholds in our thinking that originated before we came to know Christ, our goal is for them to be demolished and our minds to be renewed and renewed in the image of Christ. He also mentions arguments and pretensions, pinning them as collaborators with those strongholds.

The enemy uses arguments to directly question God's truth about us. Sometimes these are masked as questions, but exposed later as seeds of doubt. These originate in rebellion to God's Word. We see an example of this at work when the serpent tempted Eve in the Garden of Eden.

Pretensions are best described as a simulation or counterfeit created for the purpose of laying claim to what is not our own. Pretensions, as thoughts, are a strategy of the enemy not unlike that of a squatter who camps out on a property that is not his own. For a season, he may attempt to benefit from the property, but he is not the rightful owner and his presence directly infringes on the rights of those who are. Each of these is opposite to the knowledge of God. They will endeavor to work against the way God would have us think. Simply put, they need to be eradicated.

So, we ask ourselves, *What do I allow in the "theater of my mind" that is NOT in line with the knowledge of God? What might be a STRONGHOLD? What is holding strong, anchored*?

Paul instructs us to "take captive" (and lead away) any thoughts that are not obedient to Christ. Can you imagine leading away these thoughts, in chains, that once had YOU bound? Wouldn't it be great to win in that battle?

I want to encourage you to allow the Holy Spirit to speak to you and expose in you any thought processes that fall into these categories of strongholds, pretensions, or arguments. For the sake of this chapter and its subject—unforgiveness—ask him to search your heart for situations that still require forgiveness.

Forgiveness is best defined as surrendering to Jesus our right to hold a judgment or record of wrongs against another. This is a big step and rarely easy. It's no fun being hurt or feeling that the only thing we can control in the situation is our hatred and mistrust of the violator. Forgiveness does not necessarily mean we have to act as if the violation never happened. Nor does it require us to become best friends with the ones who violated us. However, it does require us to turn our feelings over to the redemptive work of Jesus in our lives so that nothing, not even unforgiveness, is able to cause distance between us and God.

Weeds will try to come back up in the same place.

We often think that just because some of our old thoughts and feelings come back into our mind that they must really be what we think, or that we must really be bad people. For instance, many things in our lives and culture today could serve as triggers the enemy will try to use to his advantage to trip us up and cause us to regress or relapse.

Don't let the old lifestyle habits define you! They are lies of the enemy! Don't believe these lies!

If you fall for this strategy of the enemy, you will find that your belief gives them life and power and you will be tempted to give validity to those thoughts, which will lead to ungodly actions and even sin. Learn this lesson when renewing your mind and pulling up weeds: Don't believe the old way of thinking when it comes back to reestablish some sort of stronghold. Remind yourself (out loud, if necessary): *That's not really who I am. It might have been the OLD me, but no longer. That behavior and way of thinking has died with Christ!* Declare this over yourself. Believe it.

Remember what Lindsey prayed: "Help me to identify those bitter roots from the past." Take a few moments to pray. As you do, keep in mind what my great friend, Linda Miller, says: "Prayer in known and unknown tongues stills our passions and gives our spirit the opportunity to rule in us so that the mind of Christ in us can find right ways to answer the situation." I love it. The power of prayer is huge in this process, isn't it?

In the next chapter, I am going to disclose secret information about my own personal superpowers and how I came to realize that I was very good at one specific mental ability.

Chapter Five

WINNING OVER WORRY

"Worry does not empty tomorrow of its sorrow; it empties today of its strength."
—Corrie ten Boom

There are some things I know I will NEVER be good at. All five feet nine inches of me will never be good at basketball. I've got no "ups." I understand that. All 155 lbs. of me will never be good at Sumo wrestling. I get that as well. (I would also look horrible in that big diaper thing and ponytail. You're welcome.)

However, do you know what I AM good at? I'm good at worrying. I worry well. So good, it might actually be classified as my superpower. Yes, I'm THAT good at worrying. It surely is exceptional and extraordinary. I can blow seemingly small complications of life fully out of proportion in just a short amount of time. I was the first person to actually "make a mountain out of a mere molehill."

Perhaps you have similar weeds in your thinking process and know exactly what I am talking about. When you read the opening paragraph of this chapter, you may even have shouted out, "Preach it, brother!"

However, you might be someone with no issues about worrying about things. That's okay. Chances are, you know someone who is, so this can help you help them. In this chapter we'll explore the effects of worry-filled thinking, what God's Word says about it, and how one can win over it and move forward in life.

One: The Worry Breakdown

Worry is a breakdown of the right way of thinking that goes against just about everything God's Word instructs us to do. The characteristics of worry and the results it yields in our lives are never positive or life giving. Here are a few distinctives of worry that will help you pinpoint its strongholds in your lives.

Worry is based on a measure of truth or factual conditions that are augmented or amplified by assigning potential circumstances to the narrative. These corresponding changes take the situation from one scenario based entirely on fact, to something altogether worse.

Many more times than I would like to admit, I have miscalculated or overspent my checking account and received the dreaded overdraft notice from my bank. It's amazing how such a tiny piece of paper can suck the oxygen right out of one's lungs, right? It caused me to begin lying awake at night, fixating on questions like: *Can we make it until my next paycheck? What if they repossess the car in the middle of the night and* put us on the street tomorrow? I'd look horrible in an orange jumpsuit! Argh!

Worry takes the relatively small fact of an overdraft and excessively and unnecessarily develops it into homelessness and prison sentences. With that, worry quickly develops into an attitude of fearful and sometimes debilitating thinking.

Worry is a battlefield in the mind that undoubtedly affects one's physical body, external relationships, and interrupts one's healthy thought patterns and outlook on life.

Have you ever heard someone say, "I was worried sick"? It's my understanding that scientists have been able to link various diseases and ailments to the process of prolonged worry. Even the Bible says, *"where there is no vision (hope), the people perish"* (Proverbs 29:18, KJV, parentheses added).

We respond best to vision and hope and excitement. Worry is a slow death. Worry creates the opposite effect.

If we have been hurt in a friendship or relationship, we may set up guards against ever being hurt that way again. We may come to potential new relationships with a built-in barrier of worry and apprehension, weakening them from the beginning.

The same goes for how we move forward in life. If we allow worry to be set as a governor on daily decisions, large or small, we will seldom get to experience joy, contentment, or gain the way that God has promised us.

Worry sets effort, brain energy, affections, and attention on things that we might not have any control over and can do nothing to change. (These are things like people's feelings, people's choices, the weather, or the economy.) No amount of worry will change them in the near future. They are out of our control.

I would love to tell you that I fit into that fraternity of middle age men who clamor for the couch while wearing their favorite football jersey, ready for the big game, but I'm not. However, I love a great story and a great one happened near the end of the 2013 season during the Auburn/Alabama college football game. The game was a thriller all the way through, but at the end of the second half the score was tied at 28, making the contest the proverbial barnburner. Alabama had the ball and set up for a sixty-plus yard field goal.

Pause.

Imagine what was going through the minds of those tired and sweaty Auburn players who had trained both in the off-season and throughout the regular season to make it to this great matchup. They had fought hard, but it seemed like time had run out for them. It seemed like the inevitable would happen. It seemed like the clock would run out and they would have no opportunity to score. After all, wasn't that the most logical and probable outcome under the circumstances? They could have succumbed to believing the worst, that the Alabama kicker would nail the extra point and the game and season would be over—for some seniors, their college careers would be over. They could have thought, *What's one second anyway? We are tired, we played hard, but it's over.* With that way of thinking they could have rationalized giving up and walking away from the experience. They could have imagined the worst and psyched themselves right out of any possibility of winning.

Well, the ball was snapped, the holder settled it, and the Alabama kicker ran up to make the kick he had often made in practice . . . and the ball MISSED its target. Worse yet, a young Auburn player named Chris David was waiting in the end zone, ready to return the kick, which he did, for a 109-yard touchdown. All this happened with one second on the clock. That day, Auburn won, 34-28, under the most unique circumstances.

That single second likely seemed like a lifetime for the players, coaches, and fans, yet there was nothing they could actually do about it. If the players or coaches—even the fans for that matter—allowed worry to rule and reign in that instance, it wouldn't have helped anything at all.

Worry is bowing down and worshiping at the throne of what hasn't actually happened yet. In other words, worry is all about things that MIGHT be.

If you have ever worried, lost sleep, or freaked out over something . . . you are in good company--really. Look at this list of heroes from the Bible who had ample reason to worry a bit.

David spoke of losing sleep in the middle of the night due to the intensity of his thoughts.

Can you imagine what was going through Noah's mind when society mocked him for building that large cruise ship and his small petting zoo began to grow exponentially?

What about Joseph when he saw that his young wife Mary was pregnant . . . and he KNEW he wasn't involved! I am sure both of them had a lot of "processing" to do, right?

My favorite is the widow who said in the midst of a famine, "As surely as the Lord your God lives, I don't have any bread—only a handful of flour in a jar and a little olive oil in a jug. I am gathering a few sticks to take home and make a meal for myself and my son, that we may eat it—and die" (1 Kings17:12, NIV). That would weigh like a ton on anyone's mind!

I also think about the prophet Elijah in 1 Kings 19, who became so fearful after hearing that assassins had been dispatched to kill him that he ran for his life! It's even worse when you consider the context.

Just before this, God used Elijah mightily to awaken the people of Israel out of their lukewarm state and return them to serving the one true God. He did this by embarrassing the 450 prophets of Baal in a fiery showdown on Mount Carmel. He became a revolutionary for God who was set to stand against all the pagan practices of the land and restore the altar of the Lord by rebuilding it! He spoke with power and authority, even topping off his revolutionary sermon and mountaintop inferno with the slaughter of every one of the pagan high priests.

I would say Elijah had quite a day! Most ministers are happy and encouraged if the crowd and the offering are strong at church on Sunday morning and celebrate by going out to lunch with their family and some close friends.

This is bigger than that. Way bigger.

I would imagine this guy was ecstatic! "You and me, God—we are quite a team, eh?" He was so excited after this great victory, he ran all the way to the town of Jezreel. Then it hit.

Elijah got word that the vindictive and evil Queen Jezebel was so furious about his display of God's power on Mount Carmel that she had ordered a bounty on his head so extreme, Don Corleone would be proud: *"May the gods deal with me, be it ever so severely, if by this time tomorrow I do not make your life like that of one of them! Elijah was afraid and ran for his life"* (1 Kings 19:2-3, NIV).

This "uberprophet" had just had the victory of a lifetime. God had shown himself strong on his behalf. I can only imagine that his reputation would have spread all throughout the land, ensuring him a spot on Christian television, the latest book deal, and the keynote speaker spot at the hottest church growth conference. You would think that his "faith tank" would have been full enough to conquer whatever came at him next. But he became afraid and ran. The mighty man became a quivering mouse, largely because of worry.

He was the best of the best and a powerful man of God . . . yet worry and fear plagued him.

winning over worry

The Bible tells us that Elijah "ran for his life," but we can look at it another way and say that he ran "from" his life. His fear and worry caused him to run from all that he was called to be. It put on hold, for at least a season of time, what God had anointed him for.

However, it is very reassuring that even in this time of fear and worry, God was right there taking care of his freaked out servant. In the course of forty days, he sent an angel to encourage Elijah and supply him with cakes of bread and water, kind of like a heavenly delivery service. This gave Elijah strength as he headed to Mt. Horeb, known as "the mountain of God." It was the place where God was.

When you get where God is, he begins working with you on your condition. In his presence all is laid bare. It's not laid bare so that *he* can see it, most often it is laid bare so that *we* can see it. He did this with Elijah in order to get to the root of how he was reacting to Jezebel's threat, and the fear and worry it created.

In both 1 Kings 19:9 (NIV) and 1 Kings 19:13 (NIV) God asks, "What are you doing here, Elijah? What's going on with you, Elijah? Why are you at this place (state of mind)? You KNOW too much, SEEN too much!" Elijah responded as many of us have when God starts asking us the hard questions: *"I have been very zealous for the Lord God Almighty. The Israelites have rejected your covenant, broken down your altars, and put your prophets to death with the sword. I am the only one left, and now they are trying to kill me too"* (1 Kings 19:10, NIV1984). Another way to say it might be, "I did everything I was supposed to do. WHY do I have troubles?" Elijah, a mighty man of God was having quite a boohoo moment, wasn't he?

Isn't this like us so many times? I know I have become defensive when God began highlighting wrong areas of my thinking (and corresponding actions). I have tried to reason with God to get him to see it from my perspective. (How foolish is that?) He already sees it from my perspective—and from ALL other perspectives for that matter.

God then began an amazingly creative process for getting Elijah's attention. The wind blew, the ground shook, and a fire raged . . . but God spoke to him in a gentle whisper and Elijah heard it.

Our problems and our challenges range from the minute and miniscule to the gigantic. Heck, sometimes we make our minute challenges gigantic simply through the process of worry. In those times, it is so important to realize that although God is aware and cares deeply about our problems and concerns, he is never worried about them, for he is powerful over all things. He has the unlimited capacity to deal with everything we are up against, even if they look like a storm, an earthquake, or a forest fire. He wins over them all in a still, small voice.

Do you remember that one of the biggest concerns Elijah had was that he was "the only one left"? God's great message of peace to him was to reassure him, "you are not alone": *"I reserve seven thousand in Israel—all whose knees have not bowed down to Baal and all whose mouths have not kissed him"* (1 Kings 19:18, NIV1984).

God started designing the solution for this very issue that Elijah had long ago. Our all-knowing God is not caught by surprise by our challenges, problems, and issues. He has been in control since before time began, he is in control now, and he will rule with power as we move forward for all of eternity.

Heaven's plan was in effect long before we were ever in need.

God was reassuring Elijah, letting him know there was a lot going on behind the scenes—more than he could see or imagine. The 7,000 represented Elijah's help, his assurance. In the same way, "warriors" with God's voice surround you as well, ready to help you.

Think of all the hard work, forethought and planning God put into this:

- 7,000 sets of prophet-bearing, prophet-raising parents were already at work, producing 7,000 strategic pregnancies while heaven orchestrated 7,000 destinies
- 7,000 touches of God on the hearts of 7,000 youngsters to be prophets
- 7,000 of those youngsters said yes to those callings
- 7,000 prophets took their calling seriously, vowing to live disciplined, dedicated, and committed lives for God

Remember, they might not have ever heard of Elijah. Surely they didn't know their very existence would be the word of encouragement that would strengthen his resolve to continue in ministry. They just said yes to God's will for their lives.

The miracle was not so much about the cakes and the water supplied by an angel, but the fact that 7,000 prophets in Israel were already in the process of preparation for that moment. So much went into THAT moment!

God will always have his way, won't he?

One thing is for sure . . . life happens to us and we find that things like sudden change, challenge, crisis, and opportunity are INEVITABLE! In times like these we have choices to make in how we respond. You can be led through seasons like this by faith or dragged through them by fear. Fear and worry surely are cripplers, and they have a "deer in the headlights" effect on our forward motion. However, faith gives us a strong anchor in the one who holds the very universe in his hands. My hope for my life is to model faith for my family so that they will see God as my source and my security.

"Let the peace of Christ rule in your hearts, since you are members of one body and are called (defined by) peace" (Colossians 3:15, NIV1984).

Two: Breaking Free from Worry

Perhaps you have been able to identify the weed of the mind, worry, in your life. How do you move forward and break free from worry? It is definitely possible to do this with God's help. God has called you to continually move forward, never stagnant or stuck. He can help you to break free.

Paul encouraged his protégé Timothy with these words: *"I remind you to fan into flame the gift of God, which is in you through the laying on of my hands. For God did not give us a spirit of timidity, but a spirit of power, of love and of self-discipline (sound, healthy mind)"* (2 Timothy 1:6-7, NIV1984, parentheses added).

We can infer that Paul knew exactly what Timothy needed to hear at that moment of his life. His encouragement to "fan into flame" lets us see that Timothy wasn't where he used to be or where he needed to be, so a healthy reminder was in order. He also thought it was important to once again repeat that timidity (fear, worry) was not the way God intended for us to live but that as believers we were suited to be powerful, full of love, and healthy on all levels.

There is something about allowing the environment of fear and worry to run rampant that causes the way we were created to think to be less than healthy.

Ways to Break Free From Worry
Gratitude

Have a thankful heart. Inventory the things God has already done and ways in which he has already blessed you. This simple action will help you focus on God's track record and will exercise your mind to incorporate faith to face current challenges of life.

Encouragement

Stock your environment with people who can effectively offer encouragement to you in your situation.

Sincere Prayer

Personal prayer time positions your heart to hear from God. So box up the stuff that is bothering you and take it to Jesus in prayer. Also, praying with a group of faith-filled believers will energize your trust in the Lord. We are going to kneel somewhere . . . either at the feet of Jesus or at the feet of the problem.

If we can worry unceasingly, we can certainly pray unceasingly. In fact, if it is easier for us to engage in fear or worry than it is to pray and believe, it proves our minds need to be renewed.

Faith

As we feed our faith, we effectively starve worry and fear. I once heard someone say, "Don't forget in the dark what you learned in the light." This is so important. We must reinforce what we know with the promises of God and remind ourselves of all he has done for us so far.

Worry is more about what if than what is—it's a belief issue:

Will God work on my behalf?
Does God have me on his mind?
Is God able to handle this?

It is so important to stand on God's promises, not what if's.

The enemy knows that fear or worry start with a small seed of doubt. If watered, fertilized, and allowed to grow, eventually they will consume us and he will have won the battle.

Three: Winning Over Worry

"For as he thinketh in his heart, so is he" (Proverbs 23:7, KJV).

There is a difference between worry and concern. Healthy concern contemplates the details of a situation in hopes of bringing a right solution and right closure. Worry offers nothing constructive to the equation. Right thinking matters. Right thinking effectively equals right living but we cannot do it on our own or out of sheer willpower.

We must work on these three things to win over worry: renew, submit, and strengthen.

It is so important for us to *renew* our minds in order to live healthy and begin to think the way we were created to think. When we get consumed by worrying and live in fear, we aren't living up to the level or standard we were created to live in Christ.

It's so important that as we act out our freedom that we *submit* to God's plan for our lives and become dependent upon him. As we age, our natural journey in life is to go from dependence to independence; our spiritual journey goes from independence to dependence.

God created us to mature into the freedom of independence in order to choose dependence.

Here is a great way to pray for *strength* as you take authority over worry.

"Lord, I want to think right and bring glory to you through my thought life. Help me win over worry. Help me to banish fear-filled thoughts and replace them with promises from Scripture and gratitude for all that you have done for me in the past."

"You will keep in perfect peace those whose minds are steadfast, because they trust in you" (Isaiah 26:3, NIV).

"Worry in our lives reveals a lack of trust in God's faithfulness. It says that, "I care more about me than you do Lord."

"No matter what situation, no matter how dark, God's grace is more than sufficient to see you through victoriously." Quotes from my good friend Josh Croft (@jcroft1977) on Twitter.

Chapter Six

WINNING OVER OUR WILL

"Seek first his kingdom and his righteousness, and all these things will be given to you as well."
—(Matthew 6:33, NIV)

Have you ever been in a grocery store or crowded mall and seen a child throw a tantrum? I'm talking the screaming, shrieking, DEFCON 5, red alert, call the National Guard kind of tantrum! These meltdowns usually progress over time from a cranky whine to a rebellious wail to a demon-child shriek that people can hear several aisles away. And let's be honest, we all go out of our way and backtrack to aisles we don't need to travel down just to see the bratty child in the midst of his or her nuclear display of defiance.

My children are teenagers and young adults now. They have matured into beautiful young ladies who we cherish as our greatest source of joy. So, when Suzy and I see some sticky-faced little demon boy in cute little overalls screaming and writhing on the floor because he didn't get his way, a smile comes to our faces knowing we will never have to deal with that again! (Oh wait, there are most likely grandkids on their way, right?) We get to calmly exit the store—unlike the distraught mother with demon-child in tow.

It's interesting to watch how different parents cope with the battle of the wills in the public setting, like the grocery store. Some are able to growl all sorts of frustrated threats at the child in little more than a whisper. (I always look for the horrified look on the kid's face as the "magic" word is spoken.) Some prefer not to deal with more tears or screams, so for the moment, they bypass threats and choose unadulterated bribery. Their hope is that the promise of a lollipop or playtime at the park will defuse the immediate situation. My favorite, however, is the parent who straps on the most shallow and weary of smiles, and then in a voice everyone else in the store can hear, says to the child something like: *"I think somebody is tired."* (Yep, somebody is tired and it's all of us because "Junior" needs a . . . well, he needs something.) Whether it's a threat or bribery, I guess the goal is to get the little kiddo and his or her out of control strong will into a zone of realistic management.

Here is something to marinate on: As dramatic as these last few paragraphs were, they aren't far off from the way we often act when dealing with our own will. I guess it is safe to admit that I have acted a bit like the kid in the shopping cart—at least a time or two.

To carry on a bit further with this theme, I had a friend say to me in regard to his young son: "My eighteen-month-old son's will is subject to mine (since I am his father and he is my son), but he has a free will of his own. My hope is that he will obey my will in important matters in life so I can rightly teach him. I'm trying to teach him important truths about life . . . those lessons WILL INDEED be learned, eventually, one way or another. When he pounds his fists on the floor in tearful rage, or when he does not get his way, intrinsic innocence can never again be. My son is screaming, 'I want MY way!'"

Free will is one of the most amazing opportunities God has ever afforded to man. It is an important part of who we are and is designed to help us navigate through life, love, and happiness. Our goal should be to key in making decisions that glorify God in our lives.

As a believer who truly desires to please God, I realize that my mind needs periodic maintenance in the area of my will. In the book of Romans, the apostle Paul tells us we can and must renew our minds: *"Do not conform any longer to the pattern of this world, but be transformed by the renewing of your mind. Then you will be able to test and approve what God's will is—his good, pleasing and perfect will"* (Romans 12:2, NIV).

Clearly, his goal was for us to understand that as our mind is continuously being renewed, we are able to better connect with what God envisions for our lives. In other words, as we are getting rid of the way we used to be, we are eliminating junk that can potentially clog our ability to hear him and his plans for our lives rightly.

"You were taught, with regard to your former way of life, to put off your old self which is being corrupted by its deceitful desires; to be made new in the attitude of your minds; and to put on the new self, created to

be like God in true righteousness and holiness" (Ephesians 4:22-24, NIV)

Both Romans 12:2 and Ephesians 4:22-24 are telling us two things: the "old" has got to go and there is a "new" that is purposed and destined for us! YES. It IS possible!

Say good-bye to the old way of thinking from the past, the programming that was developed by attitudes like unforgiveness, insecurity, fear, worry, and otherworldly influences and infections.

Right Thinking Matters

There is an internal battle raging inside of every man; a battle between his own will and God's will. If our actions are determined by our will, and our will is determined by a thought, we must recognize that right thinking matters when it comes to obeying the heart of God. Even small seed thoughts matter.

When God's will for our lives is clear to us and we begin to obey it, we will see our lives being made new and formed into his image more and more each day. Again, in Proverbs it says, *"For as he thinketh in his heart, so is he"* (Proverbs 23:7, KJV). This is a sobering thought.

The successful believers I know and have encountered in life seem to think differently than others. They are the kind of people who remind themselves of things that Jesus said, such as, *"All things are possible with God"* (Mark 10:27, NIV). Their faith in God and his promises permeates their daily thoughts and interactions and continually shores up how they proceed in life.

We can, indeed, change the way we think. We can successfully change from wrong and unhealthy thinking patterns to thinking on the principles and promises of God's Word, and allow the power of the Holy Spirit to influence our lives. However, to change the way we think, we have to win with our will and with our way.

Make a Determination to Die

One of the greatest influences in my life and ministry (second only to my own parents) has been Dr. Larry Linkous, lead pastor of New Life Christian Fellowship in Titusville, Florida. For years, he repeatedly articulated this amazing insight to our congregation and our team: "When my will crosses God's will, my will must die!" It is a simple statement that represents quite a large undertaking!

There is no room for crafty negotiations with God. He is certainly not like a supermarket parent and never resorts to placating the tantrums we tend to throw.

"Since, then, you have been raised with Christ, set your hearts on things above, where Christ is seated at the right hand of God. Set your minds on things above, not on earthly things. For you died, and your life is now hidden with Christ in God. When Christ, who is your life, appears, then you also will appear with him in glory" (Colossians 3:1-4, NIV).

"Put to death, therefore, whatever..." (Colossians 3:5, NIV).

"Put WHAT to death?" Exactly.

"But you didn't answer." Right. It's bigger than anything you might say. It's everything.

Put to death, therefore, whatever, whatsoever, anything, everything, all things. When we are dead to our own will, we don't lose a will, we gain God's will, his "good, pleasing, and perfect will."

When we are "hidden" in him, his life and light begin to appear through us. In other words, the more we die to our own will, the less people see of the old us and the more they see of Christ in us.

When we die to our will, we have to determine not to allow it to get up and shuffle around our lives like a grotesque reanimation from a lame zombie movie down at the dollar theater. We must not allow it to resurrect. We must be determined!

When old actions and thought processes die, we may well mourn them. Though we know that our old nature would only have led us to death, we may have a lingering dark familiarity with it until our minds are renewed. For example, in affair and addiction recovery, they tell you to anticipate that you may mourn the loss of bad behavior.

When you first come to the Lord and he starts dealing with you in the area of your will, you may say something like this: "I'll do it, Lord. But deep down in my heart, I'm not happy about it." He knows that. Spiritually, he is leading you through a process similar to leading an addict through detox, clearing the body of all the poisons ingested over the years. Rest assured, you will survive and you will learn to put your trust in him. Out of this, strength comes and it comes from God himself.

In situations that follow this, you will find yourself starting from a better place and reaching out to him for help and strength: "I'll do it, Lord, but I need your help." This is a much healthier position to start from—much better than the way you acted previously. You will find that more strength will come to you and God will see his image shining brightly out of you and your life. You will find yourself growing and maturing in the Lord. Though your faith started small, like a mustard seed, it will grow each time God works in you and in your mind, will, and emotions. Your prayer will go from anemic reluctance to a cry for his will to be paramount in all that you do and say: "Lord, I don't want anything in my life that doesn't bring glory to you." It is here that his character wins in you, victory comes, and you have a more pure and holy way of thinking.

Make the Bold Choice

Our will is affected by submitting to God's will and God's plan for our lives. We must make a choice: Is God going to be Lord over our thoughts and our will, or is our old way of thinking going to prevail? I encourage you to make the right choice.

Fasting regularly as you pray can help you in the battle of wills. It is an act of contrition and an exercise of discipline that will help you submit to God's will in your life.

Another key to submission of our will to God's will is meditation on God's Word. Meditate on these words of Paul to the Corinthian church:

> However, as it is written: "No eye has seen, no ear has heard, no mind has conceived what

> God has prepared for those who love him"—but God has revealed it to us by his Spirit.
> The Spirit searches all things, even the deep things of God. For who among men knows the thoughts of a man except the man's spirit within him? In the same way, no one knows the thoughts of God except the Spirit of God. We have not received the spirit of the world but the Spirit who is from God, and that we may understand what God has freely given to us. This is what we speak, not in words taught us by human wisdom but in words taught by the Spirit, expressing spiritual truths in spiritual words. The man without the Spirit does not accept the things that come from the Spirit of God, for they are foolishness to him, and he cannot understand them, because they are spiritually discerned.
> The spiritual man makes judgments about all things, but he himself is not subject to any man's judgment: "For who has known the mind of the Lord that he may instruct him?"
> But we have the mind of Christ. (1 Corinthians 2:9-16, NIV1984)

Once we acknowledge that God's will needs to be paramount in our lives, we will begin to find areas of our lives in which it is very evident our will must be submitted to his. As we pray and ask the Holy Spirit to work in us, we begin to see God's hand at work in shaping us more into the image of his Son Jesus.

Before you know it, you will begin noticing that your old ways of thinking are taking the back seat to God's new and improved thoughts, and that life, overall, is healthier and right. We will jump into this fully in the next chapter.

Chapter Seven

THINKING FOR A CHANGE

God has wonderfully equipped every believer to both emerge from the old ways of thinking that plagued them in the past and enter into new, strong, victorious thinking as they move forward in life.

Most of us like to think that we spend a lot of time using our brains. We tend to take a lot of pride in that amazingly engineered ball of intelligence jelly balanced above our shoulders. If you are like me, though, there are times when you think to yourself, *Where the heck did THAT thought come from?* Or you find yourself amidst a set of life circumstances where things are going poorly and you are painfully aware that your faith level seems low to nonexistent. You might have felt that yesterday was under control, but today you can't think straight and think you might as well run for mayor of Crazytown.

Kristen Evangelista used to attend our youth ministry and has since gone on to have a great career and a beautiful family. Recently, on Facebook, she posted a hilarious story about her sons Logan and Braedan:

"Logan, our youngest, told me, 'I accidentally hit my brother because there's just something wrong with my brain! I don't WANT to reach out my arm

and punch him, my brain just makes my arm do it all by itself!'

Hmmm. I have to give him credit, my excuse at his age was, 'my hand slipped.' His was much more creative."

Braeden's response was, 'See, mom? I TOLD you he was insane!'

My six-year-old is already claiming innocence by way of insanity. This could be a bad sign."

Funny story. (Thank you Kristen for reminding us how fun and simple life can really be.)

Whether we claim innocence by reason of insanity, seem to be contending with ghosts of our old thought lives, or are challenged by low faith thinking, we need God to invade our thoughts. He wants to do exactly that!

As a believer who really wants to please God, I have realized that my mind needs periodic maintenance. I need to start thinking for a change.

Our Minds Matter

You know, our minds matter. They matter to God. I was privileged to have grown up hearing some pretty amazing Bible teachers from whom I learned that we are created by God as a three part being. His design is both strategic and purposeful.

First, we are a spirit and we are God-conscious, or God-focused. When God speaks of creating us in his image, it is in this context. We were created to communicate and connect with our loving Creator.

Second, and the primary focus of this point, we have a soul that is comprised of our mind, will, and emotions. This is the part of us that is self-conscious, or self-focused. It is a HUGE part of who we are and so very necessary and vital to the plan God has for us as his most beloved creation. Third, we live in a body. This is the part of us that is world-conscious and afforded approximately seventy-five to eighty-five years of life on this earth (depending on our cholesterol levels and tendency toward loving extreme sports). It is so odd that so many have chosen to place the majority of their focus and attention on the body—that which is growing older and weaker—to the neglect of that which is eternal and created to be like God. All too often, we pamper and feed our flesh instead of our spirit. Caught somewhere in the middle is our soul, bouncing around like a pinball.

As God's creation, we possess all three important parts in order to round out the created experience. Calling it the human experience limits us to the numbers separated by dashes on a tombstone. We are called to be so much more than that and, through faith in Jesus Christ as our Savior, we will spend eternity in God's presence.

In light of all this, clearly our minds cannot possibly be functioning the way God originally created them to function, correct? (Or is this just me? My opinion?) The fact is, we will never change our lives until we change the way we think. The good news is, the power of God has the ability to change the way we think and ultimately the way we act as his Holy Spirit and the Word become more and more active in our hearts. Once the heart and mind develop the care to live wholeheartedly for the Lord, the actions begin to follow.

It's true. There must be more. There must be more of God's thinking, God's heart expressed in our character, right? There must be more of what he so wonderfully expressed throughout Scripture. There must be more love articulated through actions—more compassion. There must be more faith and far less fear and worry. There must be a way for us . . . to be like him.

We Are Instructed

Changed thinking is NOT automatic. We are instructed to renew our minds. God took this seriously and equipped us to be able to do it. *"Surely you heard of him and were taught in him in accordance with the truth that is in Jesus. You were taught, with regard to your former way of life, to put off your old self, which is being corrupted by its deceitful desires; to be made new in the attitude of your minds; and to put on the new self, created to be like God in true righteousness and holiness"* (Ephesians 4:21-24, NIV1984).

When Paul writes "Surely," he was reminding those in the church at Ephesus that they had already gone over this and that this "truth that is in Jesus" is all they needed for their new way of thinking. In other words, he was saying, "C'mon guys! We've been over this and Jesus is enough!" He goes on to remind them that although they had "a former way of life" and an "old self," he had taken time to teach them the way to discard them. He was careful to let them know that what once was no longer needed to be.

This reminds me of so many buddies of mine who have been radically saved. For some, the military was their background, for others, they had served jail time. Still others had been barroom brawlers at some point or even successful and talented athletes. One thing they all had in common in their former lives was their very foul mouths. Far worse than the random four-letter word, they made it a habit to talk in super crude ways, disclosing WAY too much about their sexual pleasures and preferences! However, something truly great happened as they grew in the Lord. The language that had previously stunk up the atmosphere all around them progressed into only an occasional slip of the tongue. In time, though they remained tough guys through and through, as the life and light of Jesus took over all areas of their lives, swearing was no longer a habit. That specific evidence of the old man had vanished by God's power. Though these dudes are not perfect, they sure are evidence that God still cares to see lives changed and truly transformed!

Life change doesn't necessarily happen overnight, no matter how badly we wish it would. However, it does happen. God is faithful to bring about change in us. We see this promise as Paul encourages the Philippians: *"being confident of this, that he who began a good work in you will (surely) carry it on to completion until the day of Christ Jesus"* (Philippians 1:6, NIV, parentheses added).

Back in Ephesians 4:21-24, did you notice Paul says the old self IS being corrupted? He purposefully speaks of it in the present tense. Anything we are not currently and actively turning over to God's life-changing power is bringing death to our lives. In other words, if we are not moving forward in these things, we are moving backward.

This is the part I am most excited about: Even though we have a past and an old part of us that might have been embarrassing, we have a promise for the future that is amazing, in Christ. Consider again what Paul wrote in Ephesians 4:24: *"put on the new self, created to be like God in true righteousness and holiness."* The reason we were created was part of God's design for us to be truly righteous and holy! This was always his great plan, and he put everything in place to enact it in our lives. All of this happens as we have a change of thinking. Can you believe these verses apply not only to the people of the church of Ephesus, but you and me as well?

Paul calls us to actively break the old patterns of thinking that used to define us and bind us to the world: *"Do not conform any longer to the pattern of this world, but be transformed by the renewing of your mind. Then, you will be able to test and approve what God's will is"* (Romans 12:2-3, NIV1984). Notice the instruction to not conform is to be actively and constantly carried out. Paul was telling us to remain perpetually, actively, constantly, and continually submitted to the leading and conviction of the Holy Spirit.

My great friend, Gregg Johnson, of j12.com, often talks about how he has chosen to constantly and consistently live rightly before God. He says, "I gave my life over to Christ as a young boy and have been serving Him fifteen minutes at a time ever since then." It may not be perfection, but it is indeed devotion and dedication!

It's not just change for the sake of change and it's not just a matter of deciding to change the way we think. Our minds have long practiced ways of thinking and reacting to people and the challenges of life. They need to be looked at through the magnifying glass of God's Word. Francis Frangipane has written, *"Many of our opinions about life are ours only because we know of no other way to think."*[4] Unhealthy people cannot be expected to do healthy things. So here are some practical ways to get your thinking on the right path and say good-bye to the old way of thinking.

One: Dispose of negative perceptions about yourself and download what God says about you!

Some folks have a pretty jacked up image of themselves and it permeates every aspect of their lives. Somewhere in their past, or even their childhood, a repetitive negative message or lie was able to take hold in their heart and mind, and it seemed more real than the truth. What could and should have been healthy in their formative years became odd and distorted, like a mirror in a funhouse, but it lasted a lifetime and impacted a lifestyle.

For some, this may have come as the result of years of abuse and unfortunate cruelty. It may be due to decades of wrong thinking that needs to be replaced by the life-giving promises of God. That's a lot to unlearn! However, healing is available.

A few years ago, I ran across a handout/worksheet from Dr. Henry Malone, author of *Shadow Boxing*. The worksheet had some excellent examples of common widespread lies we face, followed by a corresponding promise from God's Word. These will help you assign the right way of thinking each time the enemy tries to lie to you.

Lie: I am rejected.
Promise: I am accepted. *"How precious to me are your thoughts, O God! How vast is the sum of them!"* (Psalm 139:17, NIV).

Lie: I feel guilty.
Promise: I am totally forgiven. *"In him we have redemption through his blood, the forgiveness of sins, according to the riches of his grace…"* (Ephesians 1:7, NIV).

Lie: I am in bondage.
Promise: I am free. *"So if the Son sets you free, you will be free indeed"* (John 8:36, NIV).

Lie: I am not good enough.
Promise: I am perfect in Christ. *"God made him who had no sin to be sin for us, so that in him we might become the righteousness of God"* (2 Corinthians 5:21, NIV).

Lie: I am defeated.
Promise: I am victorious. *"For everyone born of God has overcomethe world. This is the victory that has overcome the world-even our faith"* (1 John 5:4, NIV).

Lie: There is nothing special about me.
Promise: I have been chosen and set apart by God. *"But you are a chosen people, a royal priesthood, a holy nation, God's special possession, that you may declare the praises of him who called you out of darkness into his wonderful light. Once you were not a people, but now you are the people of God; once you had not received mercy, but now you have received mercy"* (1 Peter 2:9-10, NIV).

Lie: I am depressed and hopeless.
Promise: I have all the hope I need. *"Be of good courage, and He shall strengthen your heart, all ye who hope in the Lord"* (Psalm 31:24, KJV).

Two: Go from being self-centered to Christ-centered.

It makes total sense to look out for "number one (ourselves)" out there in the marketplace. After all, no one is going to hand you a great life, you have to take it! At least, that is the corner we feel backed into.

Not so in the kingdom of God. Humility and sacrifice are the language of heaven, modeled best by Jesus himself. His time on earth was replete with actions of serving mankind by washing feet, feeding the hungry, healing the sick, dying on the cross, and even cooking for the disciples after he had risen!

The kind of unconditional love Christ modeled for us continually battles against our fleshly and selfish desires. Love gives. Everybody wins when love gives.

Love serves the needs of someone; lust satisfies only ourselves. Lust takes and only ever makes a withdrawal on relationships to satisfy selfish desires. In function, love and lust never work together in tandem. There is no cohesion between them, no playing nice. When true unconditional love slams into lust, the lust lifestyle gets very agitated and wants to win out.

Three: Get a "new creation" way of thinking.

Don't let your past become your programming. Don't focus on what was. Focus on what God says you CAN be! Things are different!

Many of us have had the chance to swing a golf club at some point in our lives. For some, the sport becomes a great pastime and hobby. For others, it becomes an obsession. With each outing and round of golf, most golfers adjust elements of their game: change their stance, adjust their grip, or even purchase new equipment in order to shave a few strokes off their game. However, there isn't anything more valuable than getting helpful hints from a professional golf instructor who, through years of playing the game and perfecting his own technique, is able to pinpoint your issues and offer suggestions.

Full-grown men will skip into the clubhouse like schoolgirls if they are able to improve their game and shave even a stroke or two off their average score. They just needed to see their game and their technique through the eyes of someone who knows more than they do and follow their advice.

Any time we need to grow or move on to a new level it will most likely require doing something differently than the way we did it in the past. After all, we are where we are due to the past decisions we made and processes we followed. The changes might even cause us to become very uncomfortable—painfully so at the onset. However, if they bring marked improvement and growth, it is so very worth it in the end. Right?

C.S. Lewis wrote, *"God, who foresaw your tribulation, has specially allowed you to go through it, NOT without PAIN but without STAIN."*

We are moving forward, toward all that God has for us and making a determined choice to step away from all that used to be. Those old ways of thinking are over and we are surrendering our lives to him.

Think of it in the symbolism of the model of the baptism action. You go down into the water bearing your old way of thinking. You crucify it through Christ, and it is immersed in God's cleansing water. Then, you are gloriously raised up, clean, washed, and resurrected! *"So from now on we regard no one from a worldly point of view. Though we once regarded Christ in this way, we do so no longer. Therefore, if anyone is in Christ, he is a new creation; the old has gone, the new has come! All this is from God, who reconciled us to himself through Christ"* (2 Corinthians 5:16-18, NIV1984).

Four: Forgive. Forgive. Forgive.

The importance of forgiveness is clear and obvious. When Jesus was asked, "How should we pray?" He answered by telling of God's process of response to our sin as well as our response toward those who have sinned against us.

"Forgive us our debts, as we also have forgiven our debtors" (Matthew 6:12, NIV1984).

"For if you forgive men when they sin against you, your heavenly Father will also forgive you" (Matthew 6:14, NIV1984).

The main stumbling blocks to forgiveness are misconceptions of what it means to forgive. Forgiveness is surrendering to Jesus our right to hold a judgment against someone, or to be paid back for the sins against us. Forgiveness lets God be the judge and jury. It in no way justifies sin or removes accountability from those who have hurt us. Nor does it mean that we must act as though nothing has happened to us.

Never confuse forgiveness and trust. For our own benefit, forgiveness must be immediate and unconditional. I know this may not seem realistic, but if we can learn to turn offenses over to Jesus and allow his work to happen in our heart, we will be so much more inclined to forgive quickly rather than to cultivate bitterness and anger over time. Trust takes time to reestablish. It can be earned over time as the relationship goes through various healing stages.

Don't allow the enemy to win by holding onto bitterness and resentment, as they are the beginning of the end for all meaningful relationships.

Five: God's promises will keep you.

Allow God to affect you more than the world can infect you.

Imagine for a moment, putting a clean slate mind in front of one of those daytime talk shows where people argue about cheating in relationships or paternity test results. What would that nubile mind look like after an afternoon, a week, or even a month of exposure?

The world will always introduce you to the lowest form of human existence. Very seldom will it simply encourage or uplift. Historically, it's tendency is to showcase and replicate man's fallen nature, not characteristics of God's character.

We see this in the opening of the story of Daniel in Daniel 1. King Jehoiakim, the king of Judah, was overthrown by King Nebuchadnezzar, and he wanted to help make Jerusalem look, act, and feel a lot more like his homeland, Babylon. The problem was, Babylon was diametrically opposed to all that was godly and righteous, and the two cultures clashed dramatically.

Daniel was selected to be a part of a reeducation process for the best looking, smartest, and most desirable young men of the land. King Nebuchadnezzar wanted to make them all just like him. He arranged to school them, clothe them, and feed them with the absolute best of the best. In some ways that sounded like a good deal for a young college-age guy, but Daniel refused to eat from the king's table because it violated God's law that prohibited him from eating food sacrificed to idols. He knew God's heart on this and it became a non-negotiable issue for him, no matter the cost. *"But Daniel resolved not to defile himself with the royal food and wine"* (Daniel 1:8, NIV).

Was he overreacting? Was he just being melodramatic? Was this really necessary? It's just a little bit of food—and what an impressive spread! (When have you known a healthy young man to turn down a great barbecue?) Even though Daniel's environment had changed radically, he had not changed. Neither his thinking nor his lifestyle choices had changed. This left King Nebuchadnezzar and everybody in his kingdom scratching their heads in confusion.

The world will always try to get you to eat from its table, but if you know the promises of God in your heart and adhere to them, you can pass up what looks attractive in the moment for that which is eternal. There is always a payoff when we stand on God's promises rather than anything the world has to offer.

> *Don't become partners with those who reject God. How can you make a partnership out of right and wrong? That's not partnership; that's war. Is light best friends with dark? Does Christ go strolling with the Devil? Do trust and mistrust hold hands? Who would think of setting up pagan idols in God's holy Temple? But that*

is exactly what we are, each of us a temple in whom God lives. God himself put it this way:
"I'll live in them, move into them;
I'll be their God and they'll be my people.
So leave the corruption and compromise;
leave it for good," says God.
"Don't link up with those who will pollute you.
I want you all for myself.
I'll be a Father to you;
you'll be sons and daughters to me."
The Word of the Master, God.
(2 Corinthians 6:14-17, MSG)

God wants to cleanse us from our past, change us from the inside out, and give us a new way of thinking.

"And the peace of God, which transcends all understanding, will guard your hearts and your minds in Christ Jesus. Finally, brothers, whatever is true, whatever is noble, whatever is right, whatever is pure, whatever is lovely, whatever is admirable—if anything is excellent or praiseworthy—think about such things" (Philippians 4:7-8, NIV).

In many ways, God has drawn clear distinctions between the way we used to think before we gave our lives to him and the way he has empowered us to think today as believers. If we continue to feed our hearts and minds the promises God has given us, we will surely grow daily in him!

It just so happens that the entire next chapter is about the truth that God has spoken over you. Enjoy!

Chapter Eight

THE TRUTH ABOUT YOU

"For as he thinketh in his heart, so is he"
(Proverbs 23:7, KJV).

Many years ago, our family would occasionally visit a theme park (using the term loosely) called Weeki Wachee, on Florida's West Coast. For those of you who don't know, it is a . . . wait for it . . . mermaid themed park, with a large amphitheater and glass pool where visitors could catch the underwater performance of the swimming "mermaids."

One summer, when my brother and I were very young, we visited the park. Upon entering the front gates, we encountered several larger-than-life statues of mermaids. Immediately, my little brother burst into uncontrollable laughter and yelled, *"Look! Booders!"* Yes, it was the first time he had seen bare-chested "women" . . . and he laughed hysterically.

His innocence and childlike naiveté came to the surface and we all got a huge kick out of it.

When speaking in churches, I have often illustrated this point by talking about my mother's swear words. (When I say this they have no clue what the next few moments hold.)

89

Historically, my mom has used the "f-word" in our home when she needs to seriously emphasize a thought. It flows quickly out of her mouth, oftentimes before she is even able to filter it. Boom. There it is, the "f-word."

Eventually as my brother and I grew older and had children, we grew nervous when this kind of language was used near our impressionable kiddos. We would find ourselves yelling, "Mom! Language!"

Yep. The "f-word."

Her "f-word" might be different than what you might be used to, or what you would consider inappropriate. It is . . . "fiddlee-dee." Yes, "fiddlee-dee." (I'm sorry I had to use language like that in this book. But I hope it can help just one person who wrestles with swearing.)

Of course, the comedy in this whole story is my mother's amazing innocence and the purity of her speech. To our family, mom embodies the Proverbs 31 woman. She exemplifies it in her daily life. She truly lives a Christlike example before us.

Many of us start out innocently enough, doing well in maintaining righteous lives and godly order. However, at some point, far too many of us end up giving habitation to thinking that is unhealthy. We let untruths or lies set up "shop" in our minds, putting us in desperate need of a mind makeover. The good news is, Jesus promises that for each of us!

My hope in the development of this last chapter is to leave you with a mind full of truth. I want it to be the kind of overarching truth that permeates every part of who you are. I want it to be a banner under which you live your life and develop your existence. I want it to be so strong in you that it rushes roughshod over every vestige of any lie and utterly destroys it.

That truth is this . . . YOU matter to God.

Don't quickly rush past that. Meditate on its power and let it be defined and reinforced by the thought of intimacy with the Creator of the universe. Give the nugget of truth its full strength and adequate time for reflection and saturation.

You (yes you). You matter. You matter to God. David is able to capture this thought so clearly: *"For you created my inmost being; you knit me together in my mother's womb. I praise you because I am fearfully and wonderfully made; your works are wonderful, I know that full well. My frame was not hidden from you when I was made in the secret place. When I was woven together in the depths of the earth, your eyes saw my unformed body. All the days ordained for me were written in your book before one of them came to be. How precious to me are your thoughts, God!"* (Psalm 139:13-17, NIV).

God Embodies Truth

One of God's greatest characteristics is that he embodies TRUTH: *"it is impossible for God to lie"* (Hebrews 6:19, NIV). Jesus stated clearly, *"I am the way and the truth and the life"* (John 14:6, NIV). Through truth comes God's promises, God's blessings, and even his direction and guidance for our lives. He supplies and makes provision for these things because he loves us and makes it a habit of loving us lavishly.

However, the enemy wants none of those things for us. He wants to see us struggle. He wants to see us fail, and ultimately, he wants to see us distant from God. He has all sorts of strategies lined up to attempt to cause this relational rift between the Creator and his creation. If the enemy can get us to retreat back to the "maybe line," cause us to fear or give up, or say "what if," he knows he can succeed.

The enemy wants us to think that we don't matter to God. That's a lie. Don't believe it. The only antidote to this and all the other lies of the enemy is a healthy dose of the truth and promises of God. If we can expose these lies and replace them with truth, we can see great things happen in our lives and the lives of those we love.

For instance, people who have struggled with acceptance can find fulfillment in God's promises in Scripture. Those who have suffered from sickness can begin to believe in the healing power God promises through his Son Jesus. Those who have only known sin and failure can begin to view life through the filter of total forgiveness, through the work of the cross. God's promises really do matter!

I remember watching a TV sitcom that centered on three teenage boys. These boys were nerdy and sure didn't fit in to the popular crowd. Between classes, one of them approached the others near the lockers in the hallway and said, "Guys, I have a superpower. I'm invisible."

He got a laugh of ridicule from his buddies, who then said, "That's ridiculous! We see you right here!"

"I AM invisible, especially to the ladies," he quickly replied. "Watch this."

He crossed the crowded hallway and proceeded to stand shoulder to shoulder with several beautiful cheerleaders. He smiled politely and said to them, "Hello." They continued to talk to each other right past him, never engaging him. As he turned to walk back through the river of students to his friends, the boys said: "He's right. It's amazing; it was like he wasn't even there!"

From this we can accurately infer that beautiful cheerleaders have an inability to see or acknowledge nerdy teenage boys.

There are times when it's easy to feel like this with God. Sometimes we might believe the lie that we just don't matter to him. It's usually in those times when we make the mistake of comparing our lives with others. We find it easy to see the blessings, gifts, and talents operating in other's lives and ours seem to pale in comparison. We fall for the "Facebook Profile Pic Syndrome" (known in clinical circles as FPPS), believing everyone else's life is better than ours because of the great photos they post on their Facebook profiles. We forget that the very nature of social media is to project to those who follow us the absolute best snapshots of our lives at the best moments, while we look absolutely fantastic! It's like a constant first date.

"Sure, just a glimpse of his glory instantly resizes us to microscopic proportions. But God is not trying to deflate us with a Milky-Way sized put down that erodes any sense of self and reduces us to a pointless existence. Just the opposite. When we see just how tiny we are, our self-worth and our God-worth can become one and the same as we are stunned with the reality that we have been made in his very likeness and are invited to know Him personally."[5]

It is easy to fall into the trap of feeling insignificant during challenging times in our lives. Insignificance is the cousin to the lie: You don't matter. The enemy wants you to think that God has favorites, plays favorites, and is spending all his time and blessing on someone other than you. It's simply not true.

God Makes Promises

God makes promises. If he said it, he will fulfill it. All throughout Scripture we can see examples of God's promises for mankind. One of my favorites is in Numbers 13, where God promises the Israelites their very own land . . . physical land. The land would be theirs, they would be free, and they would interact with him without the weight of bondage from the Egyptians or the struggle of wandering in the desert.

Even before that happened, they were promised something much greater. God told them that they would "be his people." Doesn't a plot of land seem a bit trivial in comparison to "you shall be MY people?" Possibly, but each element of God's promises work together for the fulfillment of his plan for our lives.

Promises Might Come with Challenges

God's promises to the Israelites would not come to them without challenges. The challenges didn't mean that God was caught by surprise, but that he was going to use them to prove what he said and that what he promised would surely come to pass, but by his power, not their own.

There were giants in the land they had been promised. Big, tall, smelly giants were there first. Some of the Israelites discovered this and became fearful. Others put their hope in God's promises and envisioned absolute victory, since God was on their side.

Truthfully, we have giants of various sorts between where we stand today and the place God has promised we will eventually inhabit, right? There are facts about life, challenges, and difficulties that will cause us to depend on God in order to make it through.

As a matter of fact, the ones who gave in to fear rather than believing God's promise actually said they viewed themselves like "grasshoppers" in comparison to the giants. The "grasshopper mentality" began to define them and caused them to expect defeat and failure rather than have faith and belief for victory. They were putting the onus of success or failure on themselves, not on God. God doesn't need us to spend any time figuring out how we look in any difficult situation. We need only concentrate on how he looks in the situation.

We might quickly think of the Israelites: *Their way of thinking was crazy. They had God on their side!* But, truthfully, we probably do this even more than we realize. What causes us to acquire a grasshopper mentality, expecting defeat or failure? We believed the lie rather than the truth.

the truth about you

Believing a lie can potentially cause us to live according to its definition, which includes shortcomings, failures, and deficiencies, rather than according to the truth of what God has spoken about us. If we fail in this, it could ultimately derail us from God's plan for our lives. A lie believed as truth will affect us as if it were true.

"The Bible warns us that sin is deceitful (Hebrews 3:13, NIV). *If, prior to sinning, one could display his thoughts upon a screen, the entire sequence of rationalizations and compromises—the decline into deception—would be very apparent. But deception is not apparent.*

*The lie of the enemy enters our minds in whispers, not shouts; it walks in darkness, not light. Thus Paul tells us we must '**...take every thought captive unto the obedience of Christ...**'* (2 Corinthians 10:6, NAS) *if we would discern the voice of sin."*[6]

Believe Wholeheartedly in God's Promises

It's so important that God's promises take center stage in our lives! It would do us some good if we took time to assign promises to each area of our lives, believed them, memorized them, and stood firm on them.

"You, dear children, are from God and have overcome them, because the one who is in you is greater than the one who is in the world" (1 John 4:4, NIV).

"No, in all these things we are more than conquerors through him who loved us" (Romans 8:37, NIV).

One: You matter to God, so he came down.

The entirety of the truth of this thought starts all the way back at the beginning, in Genesis, when God created Adam and Eve. The text in Genesis states that God wanted to use himself as a model to create man. What an incredible thought! He didn't experiment, he worked off the ultimate template. Adam was basically a sand castle until God blew his own breath into him to animate him. Something supernatural happened in the realm of creation at that moment. God invested part of himself into man.

However, then he went further than that. The Bible says he spoke blessings on his new creation and equipped them to be rulers over everything else. God was setting himself up to be surrounded by quality products! And he was pleased with his work, calling it "very good."

The next part of the creation process still gives me goosebumps. The Bible says God made it a point to interact with man. He didn't merely create him and leave him to his own devices. God wanted relationship with man. It even mentions that once Adam and Eve had failed and sinned, they hid from God when he came to walk in the Garden in the cool of the day.

God came down, not just to create and serve as administrator of the planet, but to develop relationship and intimacy. This is the heart of God exposed. Our God is madly in love with his creation.

Now, make it personal. Don't leave the story here with Adam. Take it to the next level. Remind yourself

the truth about you 97

that Jesus came to bring full restoration of relationship with God for all mankind.

This means you. This means me.

Sometimes, it is easy to imagine that God loves the little old lady who faithfully attends church and teaches Sunday school. Of course, he would love her—she seems flawless. However, he is equally passionate about the foulmouthed construction worker from New Jersey and the sharp-dressed stockbroker from Wall Street. He is aware of the suffering of the hungry child on the garbage dumps outside Mexico City and cares for the bushmen in Africa. His message of love and forgiveness through Jesus that the evangelist preaches in stadiums in South America is equally as strong and available to the typical suburban teenager in St. Louis. (The children's song, "He's Got the Whole World in His Hands" comes to mind.)

King David, a writer of many psalms, thought that this was so important that he wrote this verse so that we wouldn't forget that God is faithful to his promises: *"I was young and now I am old, yet I have never seen the righteous forsaken or their children begging bread"* (Psalms 37:25, NIV).

God is faithful to his promises and faithful to you.

Two: You matter to God, so he created a destiny for you.

I believe that heaven buzzes with activity as it concerns God's providence in the lives of individual people on earth. Recall this line from the Lord's Prayer: *"Your will be done on Earth (in me) as it (already exists) is in Heaven"* (Matthew 6:10, NIV, parentheses added).

God's will doesn't miss. It isn't flawed or faulty. It is strategic, detailed, and accurate. His will is the springboard from which our individual destinies spring.

This same designer of universes, the same one who created the mountains and the sunsets that sink down behind them, took time to craft and create every element of our lives so that they include everything needed to accomplish his desires.

The amazing words that God spoke to Jeremiah apply equally to each of us: *"Before I formed you in the womb, I knew (chose) you, before you were born I set you apart"* (Jeremiah 1:5, NIV, parentheses added).

We were built to custom fit our purpose in him!

Three: You mattered to God, so he pursued you.

"I have been found by those who did not seek Me; I have shown (revealed) Myself to those who did not (consciously) ask for Me" (Romans 10:20, AMP, parentheses added). God is a pursuer of the lost. God thinks. God plans. God strategizes. He is driven by the value of reconciling the lost back to vibrant and life-giving relationship with him.

God gestured our way and, through Jesus, came down to us. He caused his Son to walk in the flesh because we understand flesh. He caused him to live like us, yet remain sinless.

God is a strategic pursuer. He is detailed and methodical. I am glad that he pursued me. You know, I have come to value my own salvation in greater measure as I've grown older. Maybe it is because he has systematically revealed himself to me and, through faithfulness and determination, continued to prove each of his promises in my life.

A few years ago, in July 2005, I was told that I needed to have my aortic valve replaced due to a developmental abnormality I'd had since birth. We needed to make preparations for me to have open heart surgery. As you might imagine, that was a lot to digest and we knew we had some significant planning to do and preparations to make. Our family and friends were amazing and offered to help out in whatever way they could. What a blessing!

In spite of all the craziness that goes into preparing for a major procedure like this, my mother was thoughtful and prayerful, and always seemed to know the right things to say. She was a constant source of encouragement and support.(Can I get an amen for all the praying mommas who took the time and tears to cry out and pray to heaven on all our behalf?)

On the day of my surgery, I was understandably concerned, but I was doing my best to hold it all together in front of my family. Emotions were rushing through me like a Category 5 raging river. The only comic relief to the morning was the few moments when the male nurse walked in and said, "I need to clear the room and shave the patient."

"Excuse me? Do what?"

I nervously chuckled and he said, "No, I'm serious." So, as he and I tried to make awkward small talk about sports or weather, he proceeded do some "manscaping" that I hadn't bargained for.

I said, "I thought you guys were going in through the chest." He didn't really respond.

When he was done and packing up, there was an awkward silence and zero eye contact. I might have even been in the fetal position and sucking my thumb. I calmly said, "Call me?"

Anyway, like I said, I was nervous . . . and that little interaction with the orderly didn't help at all. Momma came in and handed me a postcard with the coolest image on it, of an operating room with several surgeons working on a patient. The tone of the image was serious and intense except for one place that immediately caught my attention. Jesus stood behind the main surgeon, reached around him, and guided his hand through the procedure.

Mom scored a three-pointer from outside!

She was reminding me that I have been pursued by God all my life and he wasn't going to abandon me now.

Our big God loves you. You matter to him. So stand firm on his promises for your life.

Maybe spending a few moments crafting a prayer like this will set the tone for moving you forward in the way you think and in setting up God's promises as the standard for your life: *"Lord, I am so thankful for all that you have done for me and the way that you have changed my life. I acknowledge that Jesus has redeemed me and my way of thinking through his work on the cross. I submit my mind to you and the power of the Holy Spirit. I stand on each and every promise you have laid out for me. Amen."*

God bless.

NOTES

Chapter Two

1. Francis Frangipane, *The Three Battlegrounds* (Cedar Rapids, Advancing Church Publications, 1989), 29.

2. Eryn Sun, "PTC Predicts TV, Pop Culture To 'Glorify' Adultery, Premarital Sex in 2012," *The Christian Post*, (2012): http://www.christianpost.com/news/ptc-predicts-tv-pop-culture-to-glorify-adultery-premarital-sex-in-2012-66320/.

Chapter Three

3. Francis Frangipane, *The Three Battlegrounds* (Cedar Rapids: Advancing Church Publications, 1989), 30.

Chapter Seven

4. Francis Frangipane, *The Three Battlegrounds* (Cedar Rapids: Advancing Church Publications, 1989), 30.

Chapter Eight

5. Louie Giglio, *I AM NOT BUT I KNOW I AM* (Sisters: Multnomah, 2005), 52.

6. Francis Frangipane, *Holiness, Truth and the Presence of God* (Marion: Advancing Church Publications, 1986), 53.

CPSIA information can be obtained
at www.ICGtesting.com
Printed in the USA
FFOW03n1224140317
33392FF